DEBS BUTLER

SECONDARY PHYSICAL EDUCATION IN ACTION

IN ACTION SERIES

A **WALKTHRUs**
PRODUCTION

Although every effort has been made to ensure that website addresses are correct at time of going to press, Hodder Education cannot be held responsible for the content of any website mentioned in this book. It is sometimes possible to find a relocated web page by typing in the address of the home page for a website in the URL window of your browser.

Hachette UK's policy is to use papers that are natural, renewable and recyclable products and made from wood grown in well-managed forests and other controlled sources. The logging and manufacturing processes are expected to conform to the environmental regulations of the country of origin.

To order, please visit www.johncatt.com or contact Customer Service at education@hachette.co.uk / +44 (0)1235 827827.

ISBN: 978 1 9152 6199 1

© Debs Butler 2024
First published in 2024 by
John Catt from Hodder Education,
An Hachette UK Company
15 Riduna Park, Station Road,
Melton, Woodbridge IP12 1QT
www.johncatt.com

The authorised representative in the EEA is Hachette Ireland, 8 Castlecourt Centre, Castleknock Road, Castleknock, Dublin 15, D15 YF6A, Ireland.

All rights reserved. Apart from any use permitted under UK copyright law, no part of this publication may be reproduced or transmitted in any form or by any means, electronic or mechanical, including photocopying and recording, or held within any information storage and retrieval system, without permission in writing from the publisher or under licence from the Copyright Licensing Agency Limited. Further details of such licences (for reprographic reproduction) may be obtained from the Copyright Licensing Agency Limited, www.cla.co.uk

Typeset in the UK.

Printed in the UK.

A catalogue record for this title is available from the British Library.

Cover illustration by Oliver Caviglioli

Thank you to the dedicated colleagues I have been fortunate to work with.
I hope that some of you find yourselves on these pages in the ideas
I have learned from you or that we have shared.

Thanks to Duncan Wilson for teaching me about... every sport.
You were very definitely my 'work with a more knowledgeable colleague',
and everyone at Stonehill made it a fantastic place to be a new teacher.
John Morris, you are the master modeller in chapter 9.

Thank you to April and Selina at Crown Hills who read chapters and,
importantly, told me what to keep and what to lose.

I love being a teacher because I love learning and because every day is different.
Writing this has been another great learning opportunity, so thank you to those
at John Catt and the Walkthrus team for the opportunity.

CONTENTS

Series foreword by Tom Sherrington _____ 5

About the author _____ 9

Chapter 1 The big picture _____ 10

Chapter 2 What the research tells us _____ 14

Chapter 3 Planning a PE curriculum _____ 22

Chapter 4 Planning units of work _____ 31

Chapter 5 Maximising lesson time _____ 38

Chapter 6 Explaining and modelling _____ 55

Chapter 7 Practice makes progress _____ 63

Chapter 8 Classroom dialogue _____ 75

Chapter 9 Teaching theory PE _____ 89

Chapter 10 Mode B in PE _____ 101

Chapter 11 Relationships and culture _____ 105

Bibliography _____ 109

SERIES FOREWORD

This series of books was commissioned as a WalkThrus Production to complement two of our other series: The *Teaching Walkthrus*, Volumes 1, 2 and 3, and the *In Action* series. We believe that, together, they represent a powerful resource for teachers in schools and colleges in multiple subject settings.

The *In Action* series has proven to be very popular with busy teachers, enabling them to engage with a range of important ideas from cognitive science and from education research more generally. In each book, the authors explore the key ideas from a specific researcher, translating them into practical approaches that teachers can adopt in their practice. So far, the series includes:

- Rosenshine's Principles of Instruction
- Collins et al's Cognitive Apprenticeship
- Fiorella & Mayer's Generative Learning
- Shimamura's MARGE Model of Learning
- Sweller's Cognitive Load Theory
- Wiliam & Leahy's Five Formative Assessment Strategies
- Annie Murphy Paul's The Extended Mind
- Dunlosky's Strengthening the Student Toolbox
- Berger's An Ethic of Excellence
- Bjork & Bjork's Desirable Difficulties
- Ausubel's Meaningful Learning

Each of these books is a guide to interpreting the research in ways that can be applied in real-world classrooms. We have been delighted by the response to the series, with teachers telling us they value the brevity and clarity and the examples of theory in practice. It's so important for teachers to have a good grounding in cognitive science so that they have not only a clear model of how learning happens but also an understanding of all the potential barriers or difficulties that students experience. Bridging the gap between research and practice is a significant challenge because real-world classrooms are so much more complicated than the controlled conditions usually set up to investigate specific concepts in trials. The authors of the *In Action* books are all serving teachers or have taught in schools for many years, so their take on the theories and concepts that their books focus on is important and incredibly useful, grounded in the reality of teaching whole, complex classes.

It's by no means a comprehensive list – not yet – and we recognise that many other aspects of research would benefit from the same treatment. Books on Nuthall's Hidden Lives of Learners, Engelmann's ideas on direct instruction and Bandura's ideas on self-efficacy are all in the pipeline. We would also encourage every teacher to engage with Dan Willingham's *Why Don't Students Like School?*.

Released in parallel with the research-informed *In Action* series, our *Teaching WalkThrus* have also been popular with over 350,000 copies distributed across the three volumes. The idea of breaking ideas down into five-step visual guides, with short punchy descriptions, has proven very successful, allowing teachers to engage with a broad range of ideas in a very accessible format that informs their training, coaching or personal reflection. Significantly, *Teaching WalkThrus* were written in a style that is context free. They are generic in style so that teachers of all subjects in any setting can engage with them, transposing the ideas into their real-world contexts. The 150+ WalkThrus are organised into six main series, each of which represents an important area for professional learning:

Behaviour and relationships
- Lesson management
- Planning for good behaviour
- Positive correction
- Relationships and mindsets

Curriculum planning
- Assessment issues
- Broad design concepts
- Challenge, inclusion, diversity
- Detailed planning

Explaining and modelling
- Giving explanations and modelling
- Reading and writing
- Standards, expectations and scaffolding
- Types of explanations

Questioning and feedback
- Assessment
- Core questioning techniques
- Deeper questioning techniques
- Feedback

Practice and retrieval
- Guided to independent practice
- Reading
- Building fluency
- Retrieval practice
- Support and challenge

Mode B teaching
- Choices and creativity
- Making it real
- Oracy
- Student directed activities

With over 4000 schools having engaged with our online WalkThrus toolkit, we know that a great deal of valuable professional learning can be supported with our generic guides as a starting point. However, throughout each book we are at pains to stress the crucial need to adapt the ideas for specific circumstances. A five-step visual WalkThrus guide is not a set of rigid rules – it is a framework for thinking through an idea, deconstructing it so that teachers can then reconstruct it themselves, forming their own mental models for enacting powerful techniques in their own classrooms. That's the spirit.

Now, having explored research ideas in the *In Action* series and general pedagogical ideas in WalkThrus, we felt that the logical next step was to bring in subject-specific books in this new series, completing the third pillar of the trio: research, pedagogy, curriculum. Each book in the *In Action* subject series has been written by practising teachers who were tasked with presenting a summary of important ideas and debates from their subject to support busy teachers in their work. We have not imposed a rigid common format and our authors were encouraged to share their own perspectives with our readers. There is no definitive book on teaching science or history or maths or physical education – so these books are explicitly written with that in mind. The books represent the authors' personal perspective on how the ideas that circulate within each subject community can translate into great practice in the classroom. Once again, we invite readers to then adapt and adopt the ideas that make sense in their context.

I have to congratulate each author on their excellent work. It's daunting to summarise and capture the spirit of a subject, balancing depth of detail with sufficient breadth of coverage of content and related debates and implementation issues – all in what is meant to be a short book. If there is one thing that characterises all our books it is that they are accessible to teachers who are time poor. Each book in this series achieves that goal – they have an energy to them and a brilliant balance of rigour, steeped in experience with teaching the subject, alongside tons of examples to bring things to life.

We hope you find this book interesting and useful, adding an important dimension to your wider reading as a teacher doing the most important work there is: developing young people so that they have the knowledge, experience, confidence and wisdom they need to make sense of their world and play their part in the communities they belong to.

ABOUT THE AUTHOR

Debs is an experienced teacher and sports coach who is committed to evidence-based practice in education and has held various roles in schools related to professional learning. She enjoys the challenge of continuing to develop her own practice and is particularly interested in curriculum and task design. Debs enjoys sports and the outdoors and is also passionate about active travel. In 2015 she took two years away from education to cycle around the world. She hopes to help pupils find enjoyment and confidence in being physically active. Debs is currently Head of PE at Crown Hills Community College, Leicester.

CHAPTER 1
THE BIG PICTURE

The purpose of PE

Every teacher thinks their subject is unique. One aim of this book is to look at how the evidence that exists on great learning can be leveraged best in a physical education environment – what is the same about learning in PE as in other subjects. However, physical education is unique. That is evident when the subject's aims are considered, not least because the perception of these varies considerably.

For someone with a stake in public health, PE and school sport are the main opportunities to support children in achieving 60 minutes per day of moderate to vigorous physical activity (MVPA). They can also learn to be healthy, active adults who have a reduced need for healthcare services.

For someone who measures school outcomes, it's important that when pupils choose to study certificated courses in PE aged 14–18, these are delivered to a high standard and this is reflected in the results gained.

For someone who works in elite sport, PE teachers are frontline 'talent' spotters, finding the next athlete such as Jessica Ennis-Hill, or a footballer such as Ian Wright.

It's relatively easy to agree that the last one of these is the least important to most pupils, and the first is the most important to most pupils and families. It's less easy to agree what a PE curriculum that contributes to achieving that would look like. In part this is due to a lack of longitudinal studies that tie together people's experiences of different curricula to their daily exercise levels as adults. With this in mind, it's necessary to consider what it is that will contribute to pupils (and their future selves) moving more and moving better, whatever that 'better' might look like. To sum up, we need pupils to become competent, confident movers. They need to know what it looks and feels like to work vigorously in a range of activities. They need to know how to keep going when they are tired or something feels difficult, and they also need to know how to support others to do the same.

A colleague illustrated this when they described their aim as a PE teacher: 'If I meet a former pupil in town, and they can tell me how they are being active, that's how I know I've done my job.'

To be competent, confident movers, pupils need to master a range of basic and more advanced movement skills. They need to know the rules of games and, even more challenging, the unwritten conventions of activities. This includes basics such as taking fair turns, knowing that first serve in badminton can be decided by throwing the shuttle up and seeing who it points to, or wiping down fitness equipment for the next gym user. This 'insider' knowledge helps everyone (not just children) feel comfortable when they go along to a new activity for the first time and should, therefore, hold value in physical education if we are truly aiming to influence adult activity levels. A strong PE curriculum should support all pupils to thrive by developing their competence and confidence – the majority so that they can become active adults, and the smaller number who strive for stronger or more elite levels of performance.

Physical literacy

Given the competing ideas and aims around PE, it can be useful for leaders and teachers to consider their decisions with the physical literacy of pupils in mind. Recent work in England has sought to build a consensus statement around what is meant by the term, describing physical literacy as 'our relationship with movement and physical activity throughout life' (Sport England, 2023a). The further detail highlights how movement, thought, feelings, social connections and communities all contribute to a person's physical literacy, positively or negatively. For secondary practitioners, the work provides vital clarification that physical literacy isn't a set of skills, like fundamental movement skills, or a movement version of literacy. It's complex and moveable, so acknowledging and trying to understand the contributory factors is challenging but important. Looking at your PE curriculum with this lens could be instructive: to what extent can pupils enjoy movement and develop this vital relationship?

How much PE?

Alongside all the things that children need to know about PE and physical activity, we also have a (moral) responsibility to ensure that lessons are as physically active as possible. Health guidelines for up to 16 years state that 60 minutes of moderate to vigorous activity per day is needed (WHO,

2020). This wouldn't include low intensity activities like walking normally to move around a school building or break time 'milling'; it is exercise that raises the heart rate and body temperature. There's quite a lot of evidence to show that this doesn't happen enough in PE lessons – a recent UK based study reported that only 24% of lesson time was spent doing moderate to vigorous physical activity (Beale et al, 2021). The Association for Physical Education (2020) recommends that pupils are active for 50–80% of lesson time. The current recommendations (DfE, 2023) are for pupils to have two hours of curriculum PE per week, however many schools do not reach this amount for all pupils. This is still too short of the recommended 60 minutes per day, but there's a dose-response effect with exercise, so any is better than none, and a little bit more than before is better again (Galán et al, 2013). In general, disadvantaged pupils tend to have fewer opportunities to participate in extra-curricular sport or out of school clubs, so making lessons active, fun and purposeful is even more important for this cohort.

What does PE look like in schools?

In most schools, pupils experience the PE curriculum through a series of (related) curriculum units. These may be organised by sport or in some other way (chapter 3). Classes usually rotate through these units, with pupils studying the same units at different times to their peers due to constraints around specialist teaching spaces. Teachers are usually PE specialists; some may teach another curriculum subject too. In some schools, pupils will be taught in ability sets, or grouped by gender, or in some other way. Most schools offer qualification PE at Key Stage 4 and Key Stage 5, and a range of extra-curricular clubs and fixtures. The latter are usually delivered by PE teachers in a voluntary capacity. If you are a current teacher, some or all of these may be true about your setting. Chapter 2 examines what research tells us about some of these issues, and chapter 3 considers the challenges of how curricula are designed in PE. Alongside any common structural features, there will be local differences in provision and curricula that reflect the faculty, school and the wider community – your decisions will be affected by your local needs and context.

Key takeaways

- PE is about more than just moving in each lesson. We need pupils to feel empowered to be active adults.
- Part of this requires learners feeling competent and confident in a range of sport and physical activity settings (courts, parks, pitches, fitness gyms).
- School PE should aim to foster pupils' physical literacy, to give a base for their adult relationship with physical activity.
- With all this mind, it's important to retain a relentless focus on the physical activity that happens in lessons – for some pupils it might be all they get.

CHAPTER 2
WHAT THE RESEARCH TELLS US

Education is a decision-making profession, whether it's choosing curriculum content, or which practice to progress to next for best effect, or whether to let pupils choose their own partner in a lesson – hundreds of decisions contribute to pupils' experiences in PE. Gathering information from a range of sources can help inform those decisions. Making links with other schools who share a similar context can be one way to look at what works. It's also useful to stay abreast of research into physical education, and education more widely. In this chapter, we'll examine some research that might support teachers and PE leaders in navigating longer term and day-to-day issues in PE.

Setting

There is currently considerable variation in whether pupils are taught in ability matched 'sets' in PE. Sometimes this is not in the control of PE faculties, as pupils may attend PE lessons already in sets from other subjects due to how the overall school timetable operates. Most research into setting has focused on maths, English and science; there is no strong weight of evidence for either setting or not setting in terms of pupil outcomes (EEF, 2021). In PE, current practices and evidence are mixed.

There is some evidence suggesting that girls seem to prefer mixed groupings for friendship reasons, and because being in a top set is undesirable (Wilkinson and Penney, 2021). In a focus group, a male pupil observed: 'There's no hiding in PE… I didn't like having to put myself out there in front of the better people' (Wilkinson and Penney, 2022). Similarly, lower set pupils have been observed to recognise the potential limitations of ability setting in terms of their progress, and still support it because they felt more comfortable in an ability matched group (Croston, 2014). Ward et al (2018) compared small-sided games with matched ability and mixed ability groups and found that pupils had higher MVPA when playing in an ability matched group. Lower ability pupils experienced higher success rates in ability matched games; higher ability pupils had more ball time in the mixed ability games. The focus on MVPA is helpful, given that we have already seen how inactive some lessons can be. There is useful learning here for all grouping systems – ability matching within your class could leverage some of the benefits in terms of active time and increasing success for the lower prior attaining pupils.

Gender grouping

There is mixed evidence concerning the MVPA of pupils in mixed gender vs single gender groups, with some studies reporting that girls are more active in mixed groups. Previous findings are outlined by Delextrat et al (2020), who find no significant differences with MVPA relating to class grouping. Conversely, another UK based study (Wallace et al, 2019) shows that girls spent more time in MVPA in girls-only classes, and have a preference for these classes in terms of how they feel about PE lessons. Girls citing boys as a reason sport and PE are not fun appears regularly (for example WSFF, 2012). Given that all studies examined showed a greater MVPA on average for boys vs girls, and that girls tend to participate in physical activity less than boys outside of their PE lessons, there is a clear need for practitioners to consider how to maximise the activity opportunities for girls in lessons, whatever grouping practice is selected. Considering gender identities, it is also important to acknowledge the inclusive benefits of mixed classes being available to pupils.

Kit

PE kit has become an increasingly sensitive issue with particular concerns around the cost to parents and gendering of options. Government guidelines now state that schools should 'keep the use of branded items to a minimum'. This should support schools in providing pupils and parents with kit guidelines that allow for at least some choice in style, fit and price point. It's also extremely important for PE and school leaders to consider their specific context in terms of what kit items may or may not be suitable. Some elite sports have recently undergone uniform changes to ensure that performers feel comfortable in their kit. Tess Howard, GB hockey player and Director of Inclusive Sportswear CIC has been a leading voice in these changes. Tess's research (Howard, 2023) on PE kits is available via open access.

Here, she summarises some key information for us:

Could you pick out two or three of the headline findings from your research study?

70% of women have seen girls drop out of sport specifically because of sports kit and related body image concerns.

Gendered school uniforms are not designed based on what is most practical or comfortable for the individual; rather they succumb to tradition and historical gender stereotypes.

Gendered school uniforms create behavioural gender binaries in sport, influence the development of a fear of 'masculinisation' and contribute to harmful athletic-feminine identity tensions in teenage girls.

Women want choice and clothing designed for the diversity of female bodies.

Which groups of pupils are likely to be most affected by kit issues?

All pupils will be affected by uniform in different ways because clothing is an intimate reflection of your relationship with your body and identity.

Teenage girls going through puberty can be affected highly by uniform, as their bodies are changing, and body awareness is heightened. This is the crunch time when girls drop out of sport, so it is key to create flexibility to encourage comfort in sport.

Pupils from minority backgrounds can be highly affected by uniform, particularly girls of Muslim faith, many of whom desire to cover up.

Pupils who express gender diverse identities can be highly affected by gendered uniform policy and kit issues. Gendered uniform specifies specific gender stereotypes which can cause stress for non-binary and trans students.

What are your top tips/takeaways for teachers and PE leaders?

Listen to your pupils. How do they feel and how do they want to feel? How can your kit policy and options encourage their sport confidence? Anonymous surveys work.

Adopt a policy that supports genuine choice for all pupils.

Add a pair of female-cut shorts to your options. Allow girls to wear either the skort or shorts in matches and training. Remove the stigma.

Centre the purpose of sport to your decision making on uniform. Ask: 'Is this uniform *enabling* participation, performance and enjoyment?'.

Appreciate that culture and knowledge has changed, and we must evolve traditional sport uniform policy to support pupils today.

Motivation

It's very common for teachers to wish for pupils to be more motivated. It certainly makes for less effortful lessons in terms of energy from the teacher – having to whip up the enthusiasm on a cold morning can be particularly tiring. There's a lot available to read more on this topic, a starting point could be Uhahne and Wijnia's (2023) proposed framework for how six major theories of motivation relate to education. Here, we'll concentrate on some key knowledge in the topic. To keep it simple, this is divided into information that helps us with long-term intrinsic motivation, and some that helps us direct attention and effort in lessons.

Firstly, motivation is a variable state. Like resilience, it is situation dependent. It's likely you will have seen pupils who are extremely motivated in some lessons, and not in others. This sounds bad, but it also means that motivation is malleable – it is something that can be built if the circumstances are tweaked in the right way. It's also useful to appreciate that success builds motivation, rather than the other way around.

Building intrinsic motivation

The self-determination theory (SDT) taught that a set of three needs must be met in order to move to intrinsic motivation, where things are done because the individual finds them fun and interesting (Deci and Ryan, 2000). This must be our ultimate goal as, in the long-term, pupils need to have sufficient motivation towards PE to choose to be physically active without us present.

Competence: Feelings of capability and mastery.

Autonomy: Availability of choice, or where activity aligns with interests/choices.

Relatedness: Feelings of belonging or connectedness.

Looking at a curriculum, unit of work or lesson with a SDT lens can be a good way to see how likely you are to meet pupils' needs. Have you given the opportunity to build competence in the activity? To what extent are choices available to pupils? How is belonging built?

To give a little more guidance, here are some things that are likely to help in PE (from White et al 2020):

- Teacher involvement: actively watching performances and giving feedback
- Novel activities
- Developing new skills
- Teacher being enthusiastic and friendly
- Getting to know the pupils
- Providing choices
- Work being appropriately challenging

Some things to avoid:

- Publicly picking teams
- Competition, although positive peer relationships mitigate the negatives of this
- More skilled pupils dominating game situations
- Pupils being compared to peers

Motivation in lessons

In *Motivated Teaching*, Peps McCrea (2020) explains that motivation drives where our attention is allocated. The amount of effort and attention pupils decide to give to a task or lesson will depend upon the perceived benefit (value), how likely it is to be achieved (expectancy or self-efficacy), and how much effort will be needed (cost). Previous success in similar tasks will hugely influence this decision. Designing lessons so that pupils can make small steps towards challenging but attainable outcomes will increase feelings of success and aligns with other key research into effective teaching (Rosenshine, 2012). In chapter 3, we'll explore more the challenges of being clear about what that success might look like. In later chapters we'll also find ways to reduce the 'cost' of an activity to pupils (routines, chapter 5) and increase its 'value' (providing context, chapter 4).

Fun

It's quite likely as a teacher you have had a conversation similar to this one, usually towards the end of term:

Pupil: Are we having a fun lesson today?

Teacher: If by that you mean are we learning and practising, then yes, we are having a fun lesson. Learning is fun.

Pupil: ...

Luckily, it turns out that learning and improving is the fourth most important fun-factor in sports participation (Visek et al, 2015). Fun can drive intrinsic motivation and is subject of this great quote by a secondary age pupil, who said that competition in PE lessons 'should look like a bunch of friends having fun' (Berstein et al, 2011).

Learning is beaten into fourth place in the fun charts by trying hard, positive team dynamics and positive coaching. The mid table is occupied by games, practice, team friendships, game time support and mental bonuses. Team rituals and swag were rated least important. Where this has real interest for us is that these findings were consistent between genders, different age groups of children, and only showed minor differences when comparing recreational to elite athletes. For a more in-depth summary, try the excellent *Myths of Sports Coaching* (Whitehead & Coe, 2021), or look at the original research papers. The implications for PE are in many ways freeing. It might be that changing the language teachers use and framing positively in lessons has even more impact than a complicated reward scheme. The top four fun-factors are low-cost and could be enacted in any curriculum model.

How could PE better prepare pupils to be active adults?

There's currently a lot of discussion about the future of PE and what curricula could and should look like. In many schools, if the content of the core PE curriculum was compared to the ways in which people exercise as adults, there is not much in the way of overlap. There is still a tendency for team sports to dominate. This likely exists for a number of reasons – the expertise of the teachers and their own experiences of PE as pupils sit alongside other contributing factors. The Active Lives Survey (Sport England, 2023) gives the most prevalent activity types for adults in England as walking, active travel and fitness activities. The data counts adults who have participated in an activity at least twice in the 28 days leading up to the survey. Team sports attract 3.1 million participants – far fewer than cycling for leisure and sport (6.4 million) and running (5.9 million). Swimming also has high participation numbers (3.8 million), as do outdoor activities – hill and mountain walking recorded 3.6 million participants. The balance of this adult participation does not align with what most schools currently offer pupils in PE, especially given that there is a continuing trend towards more individual activities in the UK and other similar nations (O'Connor and Penney, 2021). Faculties may wish to examine how they can provide stepping stones to these higher participation activities in curriculum time. A good starting point for discussion here is the paper, 'Rethinking the classification of games and sports in physical education: a response to changes in sport and participation' (O'Connor, Alfrey and Penney, 2022).

Additional categories for classifying activities are proposed, including travel sports (split into lap/circuit and route/journey): action/trick sports and rhythmic/aesthetic sports. These additional categories better reflect the distribution of adult exercise time, and the authors also call for the need to focus on 'sporting and participation forms relevant/accessible to young people in their communities'. Of great interest for discussion is the comparison of competition and play structure in the different types – some activities are oppositionally competitive, whereas others are parallel or turn-based. There's also a difference in the level to which the outcome is a focus – is the activity overtly competitive or more subtly so? In lap activities, for example, it can be straightforward to make sure pupils are not only challenged and working hard but also doing different volumes or speeds that are relevant to them. This can help with some other desirable outcomes too – removing the pressures of competition and giving opportunities for pupils to support each other socially during activities. Fewer than a third of girls list 'playing to win' as a motivator in PE, yet over half list 'having fun' and 'being with friends' as important factors in their participation (Sport England, 2023).

The ideas and classifications in this research paper provide an excellent starting for faculty discussions around curriculum content. In the next chapter, we'll look in more depth at curriculum aims and planning.

Key takeaways

- Even if you can't choose how pupils are allocated to PE, ability matching within individual classes can still support pupil learning and how pupils feel about PE.
- Girls generally move less in PE lessons and are disproportionately affected by issues with kit. How can you prepare for this in your setting?
- Creating success for pupils is key to increasing their motivation.
- Trying hard and learning are both more fun than high fives and medals.
- A lot of ways that adults move and exercise aren't reflected in a 'traditional' PE curriculum.

CHAPTER 3
PLANNING A PE CURRICULUM

Breadth and depth

The competing aims of PE can make deciding on curriculum content really challenging. And that's before access issues are even considered. Assuming a curriculum commitment to PE of 2–2.5 hours per week in Key Stage 3, there will be compromises made in terms of either managing the breadth of content, which in PE usually means reducing the number of activities studied or limiting the depth to which each activity is studied.

If the content variety is reduced, some believe it is less likely pupils will find something they can engage with and therefore potentially carry on with as a school leaver. The counter is that maintaining a wide breadth of activities can mean that pupils do not truly develop a proficiency in any/many of the areas of study (DfE, 2023). Considering that competency supports motivation (SDT, chapter 2), both of these are of real concern. There's no prescription answer for this one. What works in your school is likely to be heavily influenced by not only the next few factors discussed but also the wider ideals or objectives that are unique to your school.

Access

PE in education utopia (where everything is available, free and generally marvellous) doesn't bear much resemblance to a football lesson in horizontal rain during the February mocks. Your class were supposed to be indoors on basketball but the exam desks are out, so it's handy you reminded them to bring bobble hats last lesson. PE curriculum design differs from most other subjects in that activity rotations are essential for pupils to have equal access to the curriculum. This also means that it is usually impossible for all pupils to study the same activities in the same curriculum 'block,' as the specialist spaces can't be used by everyone at the same time. This needs careful, school-specific planning in terms of both facilities and the whole-school calendar.

If you decide to have six-week activity rotations and in January a class is due to study rugby P1 Monday and badminton P5 Weds, it's possible that out of the six weeks, three of the rugby lessons are heavily adapted due to frost, and two of the badminton lessons missed completely due to afternoon 'mock' sittings. It's likely to be hard to achieve enjoyment and proficiency for classes in those situations.

If you're in a position where you can influence how much your sports hall/ indoor sports spaces are 'lost' from PE curriculum use, then champion your use of it at every possible opportunity. Decide what spaces you can share that will be minimally impactful to learning in PE and will support learning or enjoyment for pupils in other subject areas. It's also a good idea to have a plan for what you will do when your 'normal' facilities are scheduled to be unavailable, like exam periods. If you can use the time to add value to your curriculum, the disruption becomes an opportunity, and will feel less frustrating.

Curriculum organisation

There is a current movement to organise PE by concept, rather than by sport – seen as the more traditional curriculum model. The idea of a concept curriculum has already undergone a shift from initial versions being organised by, for example, resilience or motivation, to more recent models with units that are more prescriptive about the type of activity involved. The below table shows a very basic representation of the two ideas.

Example of blocks	Concept	Sport
Rotation 1	Confidence	Badminton and netball
Rotation 2	Team work	Touch rugby and volleyball
Rotation 3	Leadership	Fencing and gymnastics

Firstly, for some PE leaders, the organisation and/or intent of the PE curriculum may well be driven by school-wide principles. Secondly, I'm not sure that a 'sport vs concept' is truly as binary as it might appear. It is possible to have a curriculum that is organised by sport, because it is largely practical to do this, but is not focused on sport/performance at all costs/elite performers only.

I have a preference for a curriculum organised by activity in my current setting and I have two main reservations around concept-based curricula, particularly where the concepts are characteristics.

Reservation 1: There is significant evidence that qualities such as resilience are unstable and context specific (for a summary, see Kegelaers and Sarkar, 2021). For example, I am very resilient when learning and practising a new sports skill. I will persevere even in the face of repeated failures. This is likely because I have had other successes, and I see myself with agency to improve in the future. I have virtually no resilience to persevering when trying to learn or speak a foreign language. I feel immediately under pressure, fairly foolish, and will revert to English at the earliest possible opportunity. I do not sustain efforts to learn at home, even though I really want to be able to speak another language. This means that 'teaching' resilience in PE may not make pupils more resilient anywhere other than PE – this is helpful, but not the scope intended with the model.

Reservation 2: The narrative around concept discussions often focuses on: 'Pupils won't need to be able to badminton smash. They will never do that again as adult.'

See also: reading Shakespeare plays, constructing an algebraic equation to describe the prices of two household shopping items, knowing how volcanoes work (we don't live near any in the midlands). This point also misses the mark for me in terms of the importance of developing competence at activities as part of becoming intrinsically motivated, as discussed in chapter 2.

I can also see the reservations that exist for 'sport-based' curricula. There is a wealth of information to say that some pupils don't enjoy PE, and that there is a drop-off in activity levels during secondary school. Given that these statistics have been true for some time, we can probably say that a narrow curriculum of football/rugby/athletics/cricket (boys) or netball/hockey/athletics/rounders (girls) isn't helpful, despite this likely being the lived experience of many current PE teachers. It's often the case that by 'sport-based' many stakeholders are referring to a curriculum that includes lessons with isolated skills in repetitive drills, (a prescriptive, linear pedagogy) and citing this as less enjoyable or effective than other methods. I don't think that sport-organised has to look like this – from chapter 5 onwards we'll look closer at lesson and practice design.

It's important that leaders really interrogate their own decision making in this area. There's not much secure evidence to fall back on. What we don't have are longitudinal studies comparing the physical activity outcomes of cohorts who experience one type of curriculum as compared to another. When adults give an opinion on PE (positive or negative), they are doing so partly based on their own experiences (Ives and Kirk, 2013). It probably wasn't cold every time they played hockey, but that is what might have stuck with them. The performative nature of PE also means that feelings, good and bad, will invoke memories that could affect future participation.

I would like to think it's possible to give pupils enjoyable, active experiences that positively influence their future participation with any well-thought through, context-relevant curriculum. Whether this is shaped around activities or something else will depend on a multitude of factors. Physical literacy can act as a guide here; consider carefully how the intended outcomes and ethos of PE in your setting contribute to nurturing pupils' relationships with being active. These aims and values are likely to be more important than what is chosen as the organisational model in creating a faculty where all pupils can thrive.

Staff expertise

'What's your specialist sport?'

It's unlikely you get very far into your PE career without hearing this question. The question to ask yourself as a teacher is the inverse: 'Which sports do I not yet have specialist knowledge in?' Building your expertise in the important skills and components of the activities you are less experienced in is absolutely critical to being able to move pupils forward effectively. Here's some ways to build that expertise.

Work with a more knowledgeable colleague

This is the education utopia situation – team teaching the sports you have the least knowledge of. It doesn't happen that often, so if you get the opportunity to observe your colleague(s) and take notes either during or after the lessons. Consider:

- What order they introduce concepts and skills.
- How practices are organised and their purpose.
- Which teaching points solve which mistakes.
- Any follow up questions you have.

Seek out sports specific training

Governing bodies provide a range of training opportunities. The most useful ones tend to be where courses have been designed specifically for teachers. These focus on the subject content: core skills, teaching points, practices that work each skill, game modifications. All of this tends to be more beneficial than level 1 coaching awards, where some of the training time will be spent on generic delivery skills, practice organisation and general procedures. These can be organised through formal networks like school sports partnerships (SSPs) or MATs, or less formally through local need and contacts.

Personal research

Video sharing sites are a great resource to check techniques and teaching points for less-familiar skills. Table tennis in particular seems to have a high number of tuition videos that could support teachers in improving their demonstrations and spotting common errors in pupil techniques. As always, interrogate the source carefully – is it reputable? Also consider the difference in terminology in different countries for some sports (e.g. volleyball). There is more on vocabulary in chapter 6.

Use department CPD time

Carry out an audit in your department or discuss this with your subject leader. Which sports do people have lots of knowledge and experience in? Does that currently translate to improved pupil outcomes in those sports? If so, how can this knowledge be shared across multiple teachers? There may be local opportunities to do this with multiple schools.

Participate in the sport yourself

In isolation this won't guarantee improving instruction for novices, especially if the coaching in the setting you join is not of high quality. There will still need to be time for reflection, planning and assessing which knowledge you learn through participation is truly relevant to the pupils. It does definitely help with the 'unwritten' stuff – the conventions and traditions of sports and activities. It can also help hugely with developing understanding of tactics and set plays. I'm very confident that the local women's basketball league did not benefit from my participation. I'm equally confident that playing allowed me to more effectively teach pupils and improved my refereeing.

Age progression: Key Stage 3 and 4

> Core PE: That which is experienced by all pupils.
>
> Qualification PE: Courses pupils have chosen to study leading to certification, e.g. GCSE PE.

Pupils arrive at secondary school with a range of experiences in PE. Some will participate in sports outside of school, some won't. Some primary schools have specialist PE practitioners in-house, others have contracted external coaches for some of their PE delivery. It can be helpful to know what PE looks like in the primary schools your pupils come from – are there common activities in all of the curricula, for example?

Many schools operate different structures for core PE during the different key stages. The rationale for this tends to relate to the need for pupils to become increasingly able to work independently in Years 10, 11, and beyond, such that they are prepared to participate in physical activity when they leave school. To achieve this increased autonomy, in some schools, pupils select a pathway of activities/outcomes, or select which activity to study each half-term. In my current setting, we operate a negotiated curriculum in Year 11, co-constructed by the class and their teacher, so that pupils have a voice in how they are active. A concern greater than breadth vs depth in Key Stage 4 and later is the trend for compulsory PE hours to be reduced. In many settings, pupils will experience just one hour of PE per week in Key Stage 4 if they are not studying a qualification PE course.

Qualification PE courses

First a caveat. Even in schools with a good uptake, it's likely that only around a third of pupils will opt for PE courses. For this reason it's important to be clear about how much and which knowledge from qualification courses will be brought into the Key Stage 3 curriculum. In recent years, some settings have added classroom theory lessons to Key Stage 3 to better prepare pupils for qualification courses – given that we have already identified pupils' movement needs, and that it is hard to meet 60 minutes per day for many children, this feels uncomfortable. It's easy to see how it happens though – pupil grades at the end of Year 11 and Year 13 are very important to schools following a UK curriculum. This accountability means that PE departments focus resources on securing these results, sometimes with a knock-on effect on core PE.

There are a range of qualification courses available to centres, most include some kind of practical component, coursework, and at least one exam. Recent changes to the more 'vocational' style courses has reduced the weighting of coursework components. Choosing which courses to offer is highly contextual – what's right for one school may not suit another. Charlotte Gallagher, head of PE at Salesian School, explains their rationale:

'We have chosen to offer OCR GCSE and CNAT Sports Studies because we wanted to ensure that all of our students have the opportunity to succeed in a PE qualification that suits their interests – some really enjoy the leadership in Sports Studies, while others have more of a focus on the practical so GCSE is a better option. We then offer A-level and the more vocational BTEC at post-16.'

Extra-curricular PE

Extra-curricular PE is an extremely important part of pupils' lives across the UK, but only *some* pupils. There is a clear expectation that PE teachers provide opportunities for pupils to access their subject after school and at lunchtimes in a way that I don't feel exists to the same extent in other areas of study. In most secondary schools, pupils have access to a range of clubs at lunchtime, before and after school. Sometimes these are staffed by paid coaches, but many are run by teachers outside of their official working hours. These can be enjoyable for both staff and pupils as well as provide great opportunities for pupils who may be unable to access activities outside of school.

For many people outside of PE teaching, this is where archetypal PE stereotypes might be most firmly placed – a competitive, unyielding autocrat who picks only the best players and ignores others. In my experience, this isn't usually the case in real life. Here are some ways extra-curricular PE can support pupils in their enjoyment and participation level:

Time clubs to fit with pupils becoming more proficient in a sport in curriculum lessons

Why this helps: Pupils feeling more confident and competent are more likely to choose to attend a club, especially if they don't already engage in the extra-curricular programme. It also means more of a level playing field for those attending – everyone already knows the basics, or the positions/conventions, etc.

What could stop this: The competition programme your school engages with locally. At the moment, that is likely to be through local Active Partnerships, who deliver the School Games programmes. Some schools time their clubs to fit with fixtures as it enables teams to be better prepared for matches.

Be clear about the type of club you are offering

Why this helps: Pupils can participate in the style they feel most comfortable and most interested in. 'Social' sports clubs in a 'turn up and play' style can enable high numbers of pupils to experience physical activity in a way that matches settings that are available locally to adults. These sessions encourage pupils to take fair turns and show sportsmanship. Pupils can ask for help and advice but have a much greater autonomy over how their time is spent. This really appeals to some. Others attend clubs because they have an even greater desire to improve. Giving clarity as to which sessions are which can help pupils to select the experiences they most enjoy.

What could stop this: Offering two types of club in the same activity may be impossible due to space and staffing. Consider rotating the schedule regularly.

Use 'pupil voice'

Why this helps: Finding out what clubs pupils want to attend and scheduling these is likely to boost attendances. It's much more fun to run a busy club than one with low numbers. It's also important if an extra-curricular club comes with a financial cost to the school.

What could stop this: Working with volunteers in any situation can be challenging. Pupils may show a strong preference for a club that no teacher has an interest in running.

Plan for progress

Why this helps: For pupils attending clubs where in-depth coaching and fixtures feature, it's worth planning a 'curriculum' of what the term might look like. This enables even more pupils to further improve at a particular sport, even if things that are planned change based on performances and pupil feedback. It's such a great opportunity to get extra time with pupils – they might improve enough to feel confident to go to a club outside of school, or gain a higher mark in their GCSE practical, or make a new friend.

What could stop this: It might feel like even more additional work for staff.

Key takeaways

- Consider how your curriculum model aligns with your aims and values. Does it fit the nuts and bolts of your faculty (facilities, staffing) and the community that you serve?
- Ensure that your curriculum allows pupils to develop sufficient competency in activities – this is likely to affect their motivation for PE.
- Champion your curriculum, whatever model is in place. Minimise the disruptions caused by losing teaching spaces whenever possible.
- Commit to developing expertise across the range of activities delivered in your context. Seek out opportunities to work with experienced colleagues.
- Extra-curricular is the icing, decoration or cherry on the top of a cake! The curriculum should remain the priority.

CHAPTER 4
PLANNING UNITS OF WORK

In this chapter, we will dig into the individual units of work that make up pupils' PE journey. However your curriculum is organised, it is likely that there will be some kind of schedule that allows classes access to different teaching spaces, activities or equipment. Each of these blocks of work need to be carefully planned – for example, what will be different for Year 8 pupils playing badminton compared to playing the sport in Year 7?

To prepare effectively, we might consider the following questions as we plan:

- To what extent might pupils have remembered or forgotten what they learned previously?
- How does the learning in this unit link to other learning?
- How does progression happen – both within and between units?

A key feature of effective planning is retaining focus on the intended end point, so here we begin by looking in more detail at the benefits of being outcome-led, and why it is sometimes hard.

Start with the end in mind

Having a clear idea of what success looks like at the end of a unit is critical at the start of the planning. It can help avoid what I think people are mostly referring to when they talk negatively about a 'sport-led' or 'traditional' curriculum. Consider a football unit with one lesson on passing, one lesson on dribbling, one lesson on shooting, and one lesson of defending, finishing with a games lesson. Or a basketball unit. Or a handball unit. Some pupils will be great by then, others will know that they find the sport hard. A unit designed like this doesn't take into account what happens if after a lesson of passing, all of the pupils are still struggling with whatever the main skill or concept was. It also gives little indication of the relative importance of the skills, or how they build on each other. You can probably think of a number of other things this type of unit doesn't do so well, yet it's possible that as a pupil this type of experience accounted for a significant portion of your PE time.

Instead of considering discrete content items that make up an activity, try to start by thinking: 'If this unit is well planned and taught, what would I expect a class to be able to know and do by the end?'

Here are some examples from Year 7:

Badminton: Use cooperative rallies to practise with classmates. Play a half-court singles game with correct serving and fair scoring. In those games, be able to hit high shuttles above the eyes and try to hit the shuttle where the opponent isn't.

Cricket: Be able to play a game of pairs cricket. In the game, batters should have the correct stance so that they are more likely to make regular, better quality contact with the ball. They should call 'yes' or 'no' to communicate runs. Fielders should move to the ball quickly to collect or catch it. They should know to send it to the keeper's or bowler's end. Bowling should be such that the batters can play shots, so will likely be underarm. Children should play fairly, identifying when players are 'out', taking fair turns and congratulating each other.

Running: Be able to try hard and keep going when feeling tired, at an appropriate pace for them. Children should be able to identify a pace they can maintain for a slightly longer period, e.g. a 'chat pace', whatever speed this is. Pupils should have plenty of opportunities to try sprinting over short distances as this happens lots elsewhere in the curriculum. Pupils should have participated in a range of team challenges, encouraging their peers and celebrating their efforts.

Reflecting on this question can lead to really interesting conversations with colleagues and you may disagree completely with my suggestions. It's likely that your intended 'end points' will also align with your overall school curriculum and how teaching and learning is led in your setting, so will be context-specific. For example, when designing the Year 7 running for endurance unit, we established during discussions that we didn't really remember being taught to run; as children, through playing whatever sport we played, we built our stamina to a point where we could keep running even when fatigued. However, this feels a bit like leaving things to chance. What if pupils don't play enough sport in addition to PE to build this level of fitness? What if they think they are bad runners because they haven't had enough opportunity to practise yet and no one has helped them to get better?

One of our main motivators for this unit is that a lot of people (almost 6 million in England alone) regularly run as adults. Running is good for you, sociable if you want it to be, relatively cheap, as competitive/non-judgmental as you want, and available in all locations. We want pupils to feel confident and competent to join an informal social running group as a school leaver, or even go along to a Parkrun, for example. These conversations helped us to build the endpoint described above and our overall aim for school leavers helped us to plan a unit that allows pupils to practise in a collaborative setting – there's lots of team games, and fun activities that involve running but there's none specific to an individual's lap time, or a race where someone comes last.

It can be much harder to be clear about the intended end point in subject areas where you have less subject knowledge. An early career teacher I have worked with recently described how they found Year 7 cricket harder to plan for even within lessons, not just at a unit level. They explained that they felt it was an unknown and wasn't sure what good cricket might look like for pupils at a relatively novice stage. Concepts and models that existed for this teacher in other sports were much stronger and they felt more able to lead pupils towards that clear idea of what the activity could look like. Department colleagues and PE leaders need to work carefully together to ensure that teachers are supported to build these mental models of what success at these (ambitious) unit end points looks like.

Once you all agree to this, the fun really starts. And sometimes some even more heated debates take place, as you identify the granular steps that will take the pupils to that end point.

Sequencing

Ordering the concepts that pupils encounter as they learn in any subject is a complex process. There's a need to balance quick successes to support motivation and long-term good technique and practice that will secure improvement and enjoyment over time. Going for quick wins without an eye on the long-term goal can be particularly problematic. Here's an example from volleyball.

It's quite tempting in some net/wall games to teach serving early on. The temptations are clear. It's relatively self-paced. There are few external variables. The technique is less complex than others in the sport. You can teach pupils to serve over the net and probably put this into some kind of fun game with serving into hoops for points, or for their classmates to catch in different court areas in the space of a lesson. Brilliant – everyone had a lovely time and they are pumped for the next lesson. Unfortunately, this class may now experience a lot of frustration. The serve-receive touch in volleyball is really hard. Even for a class with a bit of proficiency in some other skills, it's likely rallies will break down on this first touch as the ball comes over the net.

Rallies are great for two reasons: they are fun and offer opportunity for practise.

To sustain the rally, it's now necessary for pupils to either catch the serve (when will they improve first touch?) or not serve.

Consider an alternative.

Pupils spend much longer on dig and volley, including the idea that the first pass goes towards a 'setter.' They practise game units and modified mini games. These eventually start with a feed from the other side of the net. Initially this feed is aimed directly at a named receiver. As competence increases, the feed could be slightly away from a named player, or the name cue could be removed. The feed could vary between a throw, or a volley, depending on the group. Once rallies are sustained from the feed, a serve can be introduced. It should follow the same scaffold pattern – aim for a player, aim near a player, and finally, when there is widespread confidence, serving into spaces, as would happen in a competitive game.

Pupils need to experience new skills and concepts in a logical order that allows them to progress towards your challenging end point. This is worth spending time on with colleagues, challenging where you feel steps are misplaced, or where content could lead to a negative transfer of learning between curriculum units.

Year 7 Cricket

Time available: 10 x 50-minute lessons.

Intended outcome: Pupils can participate as a batter and fielder in a game of pairs cricket.

What order could this content be introduced in?	Rationale
Batting stance, backlift, front foot drive	Hitting the ball is fun!
	Backlift is crucial to be able to increase likelihood of contact with ball and consequently increase success.
	Introduces the idea of a straight bat shot that will help batters hit the ball along the floor (to not be caught out). Easy for most pupils to send in a bobble feed without much practice.
Fielding a ground ball	Batters are hitting the ball low/on the ground.
By attacking and pick up/ long barrier	We need to get the ball back in quickly.
	Gives opportunity for practise…
Low catch	Our teammates will be throwing the ball in and occasionally we will need to catch a batter out.
Underarm throw	To send the ball accurately to a teammate or to hit the stumps.
	Allows for underarm bowling. Bobble feeds become more controlled. This can include backing up as a game response by building it into game-unit practices.
Running between the wickets	Batters can then bat in pairs, like cricket pupils will have seen on TV. Increases the demands on the fielders as they now must decide which batter to try to run out.
Pull shot	Batters can score more runs by 'punishing' leg side balls. More decisions for batters to make. Bowlers can recognise that the accuracy of bowling is important.

Cricket purists might be horrified to see no place for overarm bowling here. That's OK. We won't always agree on these decisions. Personally, I would rather pupils got to a point where they are all proficient enough to enjoy some mini games, where they get lots of practice as either a single batter or in a pair, and lots of chances to be involved in fielding the ball. If this all goes well, most balls will be hit, there will be some exciting stops, catches and run outs in our mini games.

Providing context

It can be so meaningful in sequences of learning to give a 'need' or context for learning the next thing. Like here, we've just practised hitting these front foot drives along the floor, so next we need to get better at fielding that type of shot. Here are some other examples:

Dodging in netball, followed by marking: we've been practising how to get away from someone and into a space, everyone's working really hard at that now. How do we play against someone who can do that? (This one works the other way too, if you prefer defence first.)

Clear in badminton, followed by net shot: we have sent our opponent to the back of the court, now we need a way to attack the space at the front.

Between-unit links

In a worst-case scenario, PE could become a series of disconnected encounters: Netball in Year 7, September–October, then over a year later in Year 8, November–January, and again in Year 9. In each of these, a teacher could feel the need to completely repeat content, in case of pupils forgetting. For PE to truly be a physical education for pupils, it is important that alongside the clarity of curriculum aims and components and well-thought-out teaching sequences, leaders and teachers are clear about how the overall picture fits together.

I used to think that it was the absolute business when a pupil would say something like: 'Miss, this is like when we did x practice/tactic in *sport y*.'

'Yessss!' I would shout inside. 'This pupil is thinking hard about previous learning, and trying to connect what we are learning now to what they already know, this is brilliant!'

I still think this is one of the best things that can happen at school. But I think I used to leave it to chance. It would happen because a pupil had already developed some great learning strategies, or was a real enthusiast of a particular sport or player and really paid attention to it. It would happen with me as the teacher, but not *because* of me.

Now I try to think carefully about the connections that *do* exist between the skills, tactics, rules and conventions in different activities. This means that in lessons I can explain the links or pose questions that prompt pupils to think about and identify where learning is connected. Pupils are therefore clearer about how learning in one activity or curriculum area links to their other work. Also, it feels like once pupils know there *are* links, they may be more likely to interrogate future learning for other connections. They are less likely to see PE in the discrete activity blocks and more as a continuous journey.

To do this well, it's essential to map the links between key knowledge in advance. This means that you:

- will be able to make decisions about which are the high value links – the ones to really spend time on.
- can achieve clarity and agreement between teachers. Curriculum content shouldn't have a different area weighted higher by Teacher A than Teacher B.
- can be intentional in identifying between-unit retrieval activities.
- can be clearer about the need for shared vocabulary in your PE team. If we call it the 'wing' in rugby and the 'flank' in football, we make it much harder for pupils to spot patterns. This really supports explanation planning (chapter 6) and teacher feedback to pupils.

It can also be helpful to deliberately highlight when things are not alike as this can provide clarity to both the learning of movements and the understanding of tactics – there's more on the use of non-examples in chapter 6.

Key takeaways

- When planning units of work, start with what you hope the last lesson will look like.
- Where your mental models are less strong, work with others to give clarity on this big picture.
- Think carefully about the order of skills. Some quick wins might not support long-term progress.
- Don't leave it to chance that pupils will recognise patterns and links across multiple activities. Use your overall curriculum and units of work to identify linked knowledge.

CHAPTER 5
MAXIMISING LESSON TIME

There are a lot of ways learning time can be 'lost' in PE, for example changing into PE kits, moving between areas of the school building, collecting equipment or transitioning between practices. All of this before we even consider wasps and grass cutting. In this chapter, we will examine some of the ways we can ensure that as many of our precious minutes as possible are focused on learning and being physically active.

Routines

Routines support learning as they allow functional tasks to happen efficiently and effectively. As routines become automatic, they also allow for attention to be usefully directed elsewhere. In PE there is a need for teachers and departments to have clear procedures for pupils' movement in and out of changing rooms, changing, registering, and moving to work spaces. For some schools, the covid pandemic made a big change to these considerations, as pupils attended school in PE kit on the days they had PE lessons. This immediately sped up the start of lessons, and if you were in that fortunate position in your school, you likely achieved a much quicker start to the activity.

For those in schools where pupils need to change, it is worth explicitly teaching pupils how you wish this part of the lesson to be enacted. Not quite at the level of 'left leg out, right leg out', but some seemingly basic instructions can really help.

Here are some examples of issuing reminders and advice we give to pupils:

- When you arrive in the changing room, place your coat on a peg and your bag on the bench.
- Your blazer should also be hung up. Place your lanyard and tie in your blazer pockets. (This avoids lost lanyards and ties, and means that the lanyard identifies whose blazer it is.)
- Remove jewellery, put hair up and secure headscarves in the changing room, not in the lesson. (Stop! Signs on the back of the doors reiterate this.)

You could use music or a visible timer to make it clear to pupils how long they have left to change – reminding them that this is to maximise the time they have learning and working with their classmates and friends. Depending on the layout of your PE facilities and changing rooms, there may need to be some guidance issued to pupils as to where to meet their class and teacher for the lesson, especially for mixed gender classes where pupils are arriving from different changing spaces. Decide on these systems in advance as a teaching team and review them periodically to ensure that learning time is protected.

Unlike classroom-based lessons, there is no inherent organisation structure in most PE spaces – as in, there are no desks to sit behind and, subsequently, there is not usually a seating plan. Classes will need to learn and practise any routines you decide upon. Try not to think of the practice as time-wasted but as a system that you are confident will win time back in the long run. It also might be the case that in-class routines differ for your different class groups. That's OK, what is important is maintaining the consistency for that class.

Non-participants

There are sometimes pupils who cannot fully join in all the physical activity in a practical lesson. Perhaps they have an injury or a medical condition. It is important that these pupils can still access as much of the learning as possible and be fully involved in the lesson too. To support this, in my current setting we ask all pupils to change every lesson where it is possible and sensible to do so.

This means that:

- Their school uniform and shoes stay dry if the weather is wet.
- They look and feel more a part of the learning.
- If they can do some of the activity, (maybe something lower intensity or technique based) they are changed and ready to join in.
- If they feel better than they did when they asked a family member to write a note in the morning, they can now join in – if the kit hadn't been packed and brought in, this wouldn't be possible.

This last one is really helpful for things like period pains. Sometimes a pupil might feel genuinely terrible for the first half of the day and then improve later on in the day. They can participate to the level that they are comfortable with and are suitably dressed to do so. Anecdotally, when pupils are in their PE kit, I find they are more likely to engage with what's going on in the lesson and less likely to expect not to have to. For example, if given an officiating role, they seem to do it with more effort and application. It's also important to be warm and compassionate when pupils aren't feeling 100% – balance high expectations with genuine care.

Whether you decide pupils who need reduced activity will change or not, I fully urge for the term 'non-participant' to lose its place in the PE vocabulary. All pupils will be participating in the learning in the lesson, even if that day they aren't doing so by playing to their maximum. Non-performer is slightly more accurate as a term, but I still feel like the 'non' doesn't give a very inclusive feel. What you choose may relate to your context – coach, umpire, or even PE assistant all feel like a more active role and that the student is still part of the team.

Plan starters, not warm-ups

We need pupils to be as active as possible in PE lessons. We also need as much of this activity as possible to be focused on the intended outcomes. I sometimes wonder if pupils approach warm-ups with a different mindset to the rest of lessons – more of a going through the motions, rather than truly focused attention. Being clear that the activity has high value is critical – driving a culture that every minute counts. It's much easier to do this if the warm-up has more to it than 'Jog around the goal posts (point in the distance) and back'.

Warm-ups could prepare pupils for the upcoming learning in these ways:

- Recalling previously learned skills/movements
- Providing a low-intensity version of what is to come
- Physically preparing (new) movements
- Including a decision-making element

Here are some examples:

What's the activity?	How do you play?	Why is it useful?
Rock, Paper, Scissors, Chase Could be used in: invasion games	In pairs, pupils stand facing each other and play rock, paper, scissors. If it's a tie, they play again until there is a winner. At the point of the result, the winner starts running away from the other person. The pupil who lost the game starts chasing their partner. If they tag them, they swap roles. On the whistle, all pairs re-set a new rock, paper, scissors game.	Simple to explain and play. Fun! Opportunity for discussion around changing play at possession turnover, from evading to marking. Make it easier by: removing the rock, paper, scissors. Chase your partner, swap when then whistle goes.
Knee tag Could be used in: hockey, rugby, net games	In pairs, stand opposite partner with bent knees, feet just wider than shoulder width. Score by tagging (not slapping) the outside of opponent's knees. Will need to move quickly to evade/score.	Encourages good body position - semi squat, back long, chin level with floor. Movement is via side steps and lunges.
Mini tag Could be used in: just about anything	Tell the pupils how many should be in their group, and what space they should use. Whatever lines are handy! Then play tag. E.g. 4 players, in a badminton service box, or 6 players in a 10mx10m grid. Use the group sizes to help with future needs in the lesson.	Lower intensity because the space is small – speed stays relatively low. Can start at walking pace if needed too. Great for changing direction and moving precisely. Easy to progress, e.g. by saying always face the net.

What's the activity?	How do you play?	Why is it useful?
Five pass **Could be used in:** any ball/projectile game	In small teams, you need five passes to score. If you score, put the ball on the floor for the other team to start. Back to zero if there's a turnover. Keep teams small enough that everyone needs to be involved. 3v3, or 4v4. If numbers are uneven, change the target. Eg. If playing 3v4, the 4 need five passes, but the 3 only need 3.	Directly relates to play in invasion games. Can re-activate prior knowledge. Everyone is active as a marker or attacker. Easy to progress by adding additional conditions.

It's worth repeating warm-ups where appropriate. This means that pupils don't expend precious cognitive resources learning a new warm-up when there's some important new content still to come. It can also be a signpost that the learning is similar to something they have previously experienced. For example, I would play rock, paper, scissors, chase as a warm-up in rugby or netball. When this is encountered in the second sport, it becomes a prompt for questions around the similarities and differences between the two activities, or whatever is the focus of that lesson.

Stuck in the mud: The champion of warm-up games

I cannot think of an activity in practical PE where I couldn't use some kind of stuck in the mud variant for a warm up. The possibilities are virtually limitless. The pupils understand the structure of the game already from playground fun. It even sounds fun from the name. (Especially if you live somewhere it's called Tiggy Scarecrow.) What's so great about it is that the tag action can signify just about any cue you want it to. You can also easily manipulate how hard/easy it is by changing the number and personnel that are the 'taggers' at any given time, and add 'releasers' as needed.

Here are some examples:

Activity and intended outcome	How to play
Gymnastics Recall some basic balances/shapes	When you are tagged, get into a balance and hold it until someone makes a mirror of it in front of you. Variations: Could name the balance, e.g. front support or specify a number of points of contact with the floor.
Basketball (or any throw catch game) Focus could be recall catching; evasion practice; communication	When you are tagged, stand ready with a ball shaped target. (i.e. hands out to catch). Releasers are dribbling around. They will visit 'stuck' players, exchange a pass, and move on. Alternatively, the 'stuck' player retains the ball and becomes a 'releaser.' Ball carriers can't be tagged.
Athletics Movement preparation – can vary depending on event	When you are tagged, do 10 quick high knees, then carry on. Swap for squat jumps, lunges, etc.
Touch rugby Role of support player: When you don't have the ball, look for how you can support the ball carrier near you	Roughly 1 in 5 pupils should be taggers. Of the rest, approximately half have a ball. When you have a ball, you are a ball carrier, when you don't you are a support player. Only ball carriers can be tagged. When tagged, the ball carrier pops or passes the ball to a support player. Who runs to a new space and the game continues.

What's great is that often you can build these little interactions up into something that looks even more like a full version, or a more game-like situation. For some, you can also bring in a decision making element, like this example from contact rugby.

1. Identify taggers: 1 tagger to 4 free players will most likely work best here. Approximately half of non-taggers are ball carriers, the rest are support players. Only ball carriers can be tagged, when tagged, they fall (previously learned) to ground, and pop the ball to a support player who arrives and calls for the ball. Support player becomes a ball carrier and runs to a new space, the original ball carrier must now look for someone else to support.

2. Change to: ball carrier falls and presents ball. Support player now picks up and runs to a new space.
3. Progress to: when a tag happens, the tagger can either stay in the play, in which case the ball carrier should fall and present, or the tagger can go and look for another player to tag, in which case the support player should see only the ball carrier present and call for the pop pass.
4. Progress to: an additional support player could arrive at the 'present' situation, in which case the first support can pick up and pass away from the breakdown. (May need to reduce the circulating balls/taggers as the situation builds.)

Within just a few progressions we are starting to build a situation with multiple players involved, which looks like and crucially plays like something that happens in a game. There are ways to do this in other sports too – I hope you enjoy thinking of more SITM variations to use in your lessons.

Transitions in lessons

Aiming for 80% active time in lessons takes planning and training. By training, I mean how a teacher prepares pupils to transition quickly in lessons. The reasons for each instruction/organisational method you choose will initially need to be clearly explained with regular reminders. Over time, classes will become more used to how things are done.

Group sizes

Think carefully about the optimum group size needed for your most 'important' practice in a particular lesson. If it's four, avoid the need for pupils to work in a group of three earlier in the lesson. Map out the necessary changes such that they are minimal and easy to navigate.

Example 1: Basketball lesson where final practice is 3v2 with one person acting as a 'dribble coach', approximately 30 pupils.

Part of lesson	Group size	Organisation
Starter	2	'Find a partner you can work well with in PE.' Or sometimes: 'Find a partner who is similar to you in PE.'
Practice 1	2	Assuming there has been no difficulties (e.g. behaviour issues), stay with the same partner.
Practice 2	6	'In your pair, find two other pairs, and sit behind the yellow line.'

Example 2: Netball lesson, where the second half of the lesson is a full game, approximately 28 pupils.

Part of lesson	Group size	Organisation
Starter	2	'Find a partner you can work well with.'
Practice 1	4	'In your pair, find another pair.'
Practice 2	7	'In your four line up one behind the other behind the yellow line. Now can the front person in each line take a big step forward. You are the blue team, collect the bibs and stand in the centre third.'
		This can now be repeated to organise the remaining three teams. Note that there is a need to scan the first team that you identify – the ones who put themselves at the front of the line, as this can sometimes hold a disproportionate number of the stronger players. This is especially true if you were to play the front of the line team against the back of the line team. Interesting social structure, even though it's likely that pupils left to their own devices got into relatively ability-matched fours in the first place.

'I was always the last person picked in PE.'

If we approach decisions in school with educational reasons in mind, there is no need for there to be a situation in PE lessons where pupil captains pick teams. There are a lot of other ways to get pupils into teams or groups – some are already described in the previous table. Most of these are based on pupils making an initial identification of a partner. Some pupils find this hard and may need support to find working groups. Have a plan for this generically, such as, 'If you can't find a partner straight away, walk over to me to get organised', and more specifically, by checking in with particular pupils before or during the lesson. Alternatively, you can put pupils into groups and teams yourself, either 'on the fly' in the lesson, or with lists in the changing rooms. The advantages of grouping pupils yourself can be significant – you may wish to ability-match or ability mix to best support what is being learned. It's likely both approaches will be needed at some point and it's key to obtain a balance of pupil selection and occasions where you think learning will be better if you choose. Keep in mind that 'working with friends' is commonly listed as being high value to pupils in PE, especially for girls (YST, Girls Active 2023).

Top tip

If you are putting pupils into groups, whether by giving them a number or colour, have the pupil repeat it back to you as you say it to them. I have seen teachers give out numbers to put pupils into teams a lot of times. Often Team 1 has 7 players, Team 2 has 5 players, and so on. Pupils either aren't sure or manipulate the fact that it was *possible* for them to have been unsure and go to their preferred group. Getting them to say the number back means that it was definitely understood, and now we have this mini verbal contract which they don't seem to break.

Precision instructions

There's a need for precision in both the ordering of information and the information itself. For example, if the first content given is the number of the group, very commonly pupils will begin thinking about who they will work with, and the second part of the instruction (where to stand when ready) is lost. Withholding the number in the group until the end prevents this mental or enacted organisation before you are completely ready for it to happen.

You will notice that the previous examples of group transitions are precise around where to sit or stand. This is important for a few reasons:

- Teachers can see that pupils are organised and ready
- Teachers can position to prevent other distractions (sun, strimming/mowing, other groups working)
- Teachers have the best view of the demonstration

As part of 'training' your classes to transition quickly, it's worth explaining to pupils why you are being so precise about where they should sit or stand. Luckily this is a fairness thing, so most get on board with it very quickly. (Children can spot injustice a mile off.) For example, 'I'm asking you to stand behind the yellow line so that everyone has a good view of the next practice. This means that everyone has a fair chance to learn well, do their best and help their friends practice.'

It also helps to be very clear about the expectations for how pupils will be conducting themselves during this time. We want the transitions to happen quickly so that practice time is maximised – it's important to convey that need warmly and positively. Gestures also help to clearly indicate where pupils should be and any other actions they need to take, like storing equipment.

For example:

'Everyone needs to sit in a line in their group of 4. One behind the other, with your equipment placed at the front of the line.'	Four stages of escalations here after the initial instruction:
'Thanks to this group – all ready to listen with equipment at the front, and to this group, well done.'	- Praise to those who act straight away.
'Thanks to everyone who is ready.'	- General praise, making it sound like most people are on board with this; subtext: you should be too. This is a social nudge.
'If your equipment is not at the front, place it there now.'	- General instruction repeat of a problem you have seen when scanning. Pupils do not feel targeted or are being called out in front of their peers.
'Adam, face the front, and pass your racket to Rehan. Thank you.'	- Specific to one or two pupils who have not yet complied.

There's more on explaining, demonstrating and choosing practices later in the book, so for now it's enough to say that the demonstration, explanation and discussion should be well-planned, such that it is effective without overloading pupils. Sometimes class Q&A will lead to more interesting points to discuss, which can be helpful and offer additional knowledge and challenge for pupils – we'll explore this more in chapter 8. Even when the discussion is good quality, we must still keep focus on active time in the lesson – remember we're aiming for 50–80% in each lesson. A strategy to help this all keep to time is to pre-teach one group the next practice.

This can be a very time efficient way to move a class forward. It allows for a group being ahead of their classmates (caveat to follow on that one), and for a demonstration to be 'practised' in advance so that it is performed more fluently. Explain the next practice task to one of the working groups and have them run it through a few times with some feedback from you.

Ask them to keep going with the practice, and when the class/the demo group are ready, call everyone over.

'You carry on with the practice please, I'm inviting your friends over to have a look at your fantastic work. Everyone, pause your work and stand behind the yellow line so that you can see the group practising here. Thank you. Watch carefully. Be ready to tell us what you notice about their practice.' You might give them something specific to look for or think about, for example: 'Watch what Inaya is doing – what are all the ways she is supporting her team to attack?'

This can work really well for groups where behaviour is challenging, or who are particularly chatty – the waiting time is shorter because the demo is already underway and you can use dialogue like: 'Your classmates have prepared this demonstration – respect your friends by paying attention.' You can then cold call, or think pair share to elicit the important points from the class, adding any key details that will allow the other working groups to reproduce the practice. The caveat from earlier is to avoid always using the same groups/pupils as the demonstrators. This is to be avoided anyway in PE, as research indicates that often pupils perceive that PE teachers spend more time with or talking to more able pupils.

Practice selection

It's really easy to find drills/practices for different sports now. There are thousands available to watch on the internet – much easier than translating small diagrams with crosses and dots to what it looks like in the real world. It can be very tempting to see a great practice for a sport and think, 'Great, I'll use that next time I teach x'. A very real and tempting 'magpie effect' exists when it comes to practice selection! Instead consider the following questions:

Does it solve a problem pupils have?

Will this practice help your pupils get better at something they are finding hard or are not yet able to do consistently? Will this practice help motivate your pupils to work harder, or provide context for the next steps in their learning? If the answer isn't yes to any of these questions, then the practice isn't a good selection right now. It might be fun and active, but it's likely there's something fun and active that also moves pupils forwards.

What is the cone commitment?

Is this practice easy to set up? Some sports coaches love cones. Practices are set up requiring all kinds of complex layouts, colour coding, etc. Sometimes these last a matter of minutes, and then a whole new arrangement is required. Life is short and PE lessons are even shorter. I urge conservatism with cone usage and equipment set up in general.

Ideally we are aiming for simple layouts that can be easily recreated by pupils if they are in small working groups. For example, 'Look at this square. I have two cones on the white lines. I made a square that is ten big steps each side with the other two cones.'

It is even better if you can plan the transitions such that the layout can be retained for the whole lesson with only minimal adjustments, just like with group sizes earlier in the chapter.

NB. These days I don't do much coaching outside of school, where there is definitely an over-commitment to cones. The most common time I see elaborate cone set ups is in interview lessons. If you are preparing for an interview, consider how realistic your set-up is. It might be your favourite practice, and on the interview lesson there's sometimes a bit of preparation time. Will you still be able to set it up like that on a wet Wednesday when you're running to your lesson from Year 9 break duty?

Does it maximise pupil involvement?

I have a couple of really effective practices that I will never use in lessons because pupils do not get enough turns. They will be inactive for too long and not experience sufficient practice repetitions. These are practices that sometimes work at after school clubs, or where there's a high value to watching others do it – like a set play in a GCSE netball lesson – but are otherwise absolute curriculum lesson rejects. Waiting in line for a turn isn't fun. Pupils will move forward in their learning slower without practice, and the 50–80% active time aim will become even harder to achieve. Ideally pupils shouldn't be waiting for more than 2–3 others to take a turn before it is their 'go'.

What prior knowledge is needed to perform this?

The pupils might be about to practise something that is the next logical step for them, but if to do that they need to receive a particular pass, feed or interact with another pupil in a new or more challenging way the task could be less effective than intended. Minimising the complexity of other aspects of the practice could help or check for any other necessary skills/ movements in a warm-up task.

Is it easy to explain, demonstrate and replicate?

This is probably the most likely situation where sunk cost bias could happen in PE. The teacher has a 'really great' practice which happens to be a little more complex than some others the class have been doing. Maybe the teacher has seen it done effectively in a different context. The drill is demo-ed, the demo doesn't go that well; it takes longer than usual or is a poor quality model. The understanding check takes longer than usual. The groups go to practice – some groups have not got the practice operating smoothly. Some are functioning to an OK level, but the practice still isn't working on the desired outcome. The teacher thinks either:

- 'We've spent so much time on this, we need to get it right' and perseveres with it. Maybe it works, maybe it doesn't. Was it worth the time cost if it does? Will it be used again?
- Or, 'scrap this, let's do it another way', which results in time lost.

Some practices are worth investing in because the procedural knowledge is worth retaining for pupils to use again and again.

Here's an example:

A couple of years ago I decided to teach a Year 7 boys group a 4v2 possession game, or keep-away, in football. The class are extremely enthusiastic in PE lessons, and really value game-based activities. The idea was that by teaching a 4v2 keep-away as a base unit, we would then be able to add other constraints without a need to re-explain the main ways of playing. Here's the rules we used:

Attackers (4, no bibs):

Get a point each, every time four passes are made with no defender scoring a point.

If the ball goes out of play, attackers always re-start.

Ball stays on the floor.

Defenders (2, bibs):

Get a point if they touch the ball; they are the nearest defender when the ball goes out; they stop the ball.

When three (personal) points are reached, the bib can be given to whoever they like.

Be fair, make sure everyone gets the same amount of turns to be a defender.

This worked for this class. For other classes a 4v1 or 3v1 may be more appropriate. From whatever base unit you choose, changes could be made to support other learning outcomes or make the game suitable for the experience of the group:

Adjust size of area to make it harder/easier for either side.

Attackers have limited touches.

Attackers must work the ball through a particular area/to a particular player.

Defenders can complete a pass to each other for instant win (transition after regaining possession).

Defenders can't press a particular player.

Defenders gain extra points for passing/dribbling the ball out of a particular target area.

A main win of this is that in a number of sports I can now say to this class, 'Set-up a 4v2 keep-away using our normal rules.' As we have done this over time, initially with checks for understanding, pupils now retrieve the information quickly, find a suitable group, collect the four cones, two bibs and one ball needed and get underway. The only additional information from me might relate to the size of the space needed. Depending on where we are working, there might be marked lines meaning no cones are needed. I can then pause the practice as needed to vary the constraints. It's much more likely that pupils can focus on these constraints too. They don't have to think about how to organise the keep-away game as they have done it before – so precious attention can now be re-directed to whatever we are learning that day.

Turn taking

Some children will take the first turn every time, or try to. This can create unfairness in the volume of practice time pupils get in lessons. To support in particular those pupils who find it hard to challenge their peers, there's a few steps we can take:

If swaps or turns are timed, actually time them, don't just guess.

If swaps/turns are pupil regulated, be very clear about how many should happen. If you don't think turns are being taken, intervene with a whistle and clear instruction: 'If you haven't changed jobs yet, change now.' Warmly praise where you see pupils taking fair goes, or giving an extra turn to someone in their group who is finding something harder.

It can be tricky to balance how many pupils can be safely working at any one time, especially if you are in a school where indoor space is limited. Avoiding having lines or groups of pupils waiting for their turn is essential. In most activities, groups of 2–4 are possible for most tasks. This holds true even for sports like fencing or contact rugby if the layout of the lesson has been planned with care. For the latter, you could have more than one game by switching to Touch whenever you are not officiating that mini game, and circulating between the mini games to give each group of players a relevant experience. Alternatively, you could position to see all mini-games, and reduce the pace of the game to walking pace, or have players on their knees.

Where wait time is unavoidable, e.g. to use a piece of specialist equipment like a gymnastic vault or long jump pit, set up some other task(s) that can be done safely between turns, or as part of a circuit to increase practice time. This also supports pupils in making good behaviour choices – waiting time is often where silly, niggly behaviours happen.

Checking for task understanding

There is so much potential for time to be lost in PE lessons – changing, collecting equipment, moving to the work space all steal learning and practice time. Then in the lesson we need groups of different numbers, cones in particular places, bibs, helmets, mats, pupils to move safely whilst others are exercising, and any number of other permutations. Aiming for 50-80% of time in MPA or better means that efficient clarity around practice tasks is essential. Earlier, practice selection was discussed, with particular emphasis on a practice not being so complex that it distracts from the intended learning. In getting practices underway, closed questions are useful to gauge pupils' readiness.

Example 1. Pupils have been shown a practice involving two players trying to make successful passes to each other whilst being man-marked. This could happen in netball, basketball or handball and is quite a difficult practice.

Q: What will you do first? [Pause for thinking time] Jenny?

A: Find a group of 4.

Q: Thank you, Jenny. If you cannot find a group of 4, please find me. What equipment will you collect? [Pause for thinking time] Akash?

A: Two bibs and a ball.

Q: Smashing, you can decide who will get what in your group. What else do you need to know to get started?

This last question can be important. The main way to know if a class have 'got' the shape and structure of the practice is to see them doing it, so there's a real focus on getting underway. Here, we try to eliminate obstacles to getting started. This is much more effective than 'any questions?' as the question structure legitimises future questions. You can then deal with any questions you get and allow the pupils to start.

I don't get it

This is a difficult question for teachers of any subject. You don't get what? Try to avoid repeating the entire explanation a second time. This could be time consuming and still not solve the problem. I prefer to respond to statements like 'I don't get it' with 'Ask me a question that will help you to understand or get started'. This has a couple of benefits:

- If the pupil can identify a particular problem, you can usually deal with it quickly and easily.
- From the question, you may be able to assess whether this is a difficulty that will affect multiple pupils/groups or whether some can begin work while you provide support to others.
- If 'I don't get it' was a way of avoiding thinking hard, there's now a need to think hard to ask a question. Sometimes pupils will then decide it's easier just to think about the task you gave them in the first instance.

Key takeaways

- Plan routines to fit your faculty and invest time in teaching them to pupils.
- The warm up is a key part of the lesson – maximise it's value by making it specific to the lesson outcomes.
- Consider carefully how to minimise transitional periods in lessons by maintaining group sizes/equipment set ups through multiple practices.

- Try to re-use practices so that pupils can get to work quickly, and can focus on the concept being learned, rather than learning the practice itself.
- Before sending pupils off to work, check they have understood what to do next. It's much easier to do this in a small space than once they are spread over the whole work area.

CHAPTER 6
EXPLAINING AND MODELLING

It will take careful thought to plan out these teaching sequences for movement skills. Most PE teachers will have a significant volume of experience in movement activities as a participant in addition to their time spent teaching, coaching, or leading movement. They would likely have been strong practical performers in their PE lessons as a pupil, even if they no longer play or train. (At a recent head of department PE meeting I attended, only about a third of the attendees said they were still playing a sport). Whether explicitly or implicitly, PE teachers will have developed movement skills and habits that allow for less effortful, more fluent performances. This 'curse of knowledge' makes it hard to remember a time when you were more novice-like (Heath and Heath, 2007) and less fluent – less 'natural' looking when playing sports. It can be very hard to break these movement skills into constituent parts, and even harder to identify some of the underlying techniques that have become 'natural' or automatic for the teacher but require teaching and practise for pupils to achieve a level of fluency.

Consider an interception in netball. For an interception to happen in a game, the player should be ready to move with weight through the balls of their feet, feet apart, knees bent, with a relative evenness of weight distribution between the feet.

They should be positioned appropriately, e.g. such that they can see the player they are marking and the play.

They should scan the court for the position of opponents/position of teammates.

They should match the pattern of players on the court/position of the ball to other experiences of game play from memory.

They need to make a prediction about what might happen next.

They should move purposefully towards the ball.

There's a lot going on there and we haven't even mentioned preparing to catch the ball, judging the flight of the ball, catching, or organising feet for subsequent landing/running pass. As practitioners, we need to explicitly build small blocks of movements and game experiences, allowing pupils to gain fluency and a memory bank of game play.

Crucially, we will have to show pupils what effective movements look like, explain how to replicate these, and give pupils opportunities to practise, refine and problem solve movement solutions.

Introducing a new movement skill

When introducing pupils to a new skill, there are a number of factors to consider, starting with any prior knowledge that they need to be successful.

What are the prerequisites to do this?

It could be that the new skill to be learned is made up of new body positions and movements. Many 'new' skills though will contain elements of previously practised techniques. Consider if it is possible to check for/reactivate this prior knowledge through a warm-up activity that requires pupils to recall and reproduce the previously learned movement without re-instruction. The accuracy of the reproduction will then allow for a decision to be made – is further practice of an earlier technique needed, or is the performance secure enough to underpin the next step?

How could this be simplified?

To achieve the most accessible version of a new skill, consider how to control some or all of the following:

- The movement(s) to be made
- Working area
- Time available/pacing
- Opposition

We will explore this further in chapter 7, when we look at designing and using practice tasks. A key idea here is simplify, not isolate.

What are all the ways that pupils can engage with your explanation?

In some cases, it may be possible for pupils to be doing the new movement as you are describing it. Usually though, at a first encounter the class are likely to be sitting or standing whilst listening to and watching the explanation and demonstration. This is because it is impractical and difficult for them to be trying something new, whilst also doing the watching and listening. Here are some ways you could ensure that pupils' attention is directed to important features of the explanation.

- Signpost in advance that there are links to previously learned skills, so that pupils can listen/look for these.
- Ask questions during the explanation to check pupils are following.
- Use touch to illustrate a point you are making. This could be giving class members the opportunity to touch equipment, or the most effective way I see this working in lessons is when I ask pupils to touch the part of their body that I am asking them to use. For example, when teaching how to stop the ball in football, I ask classes to touch the inside of their own foot, with the narration that this is where you should feel the ball when you are stopping the football. Same with fingertips in basketball dribbling, or a volleyball volley. Classes that I have taught over time don't see this as strange and my feeling is that it helps them remember in future lessons how the movement works, as well as giving a good starting point when skills are new. I've since learned that this likely relates to the idea of embodied cognition (see Turner et al 2020 for more on this).

What are the common errors?

Highlighting the common errors up front can be very helpful – you are legitimising them happening. Embracing these possible failures as part of the learning process, and letting pupils know that they are not alone in experiencing that particular challenge means that pupils are more likely to continue investing effort in learning. Explaining and showing the likely mistakes also helps pupils to spot them happening in their own and others' performances. This supports pupils in becoming effective peer coaches, discussed in chapter 8. In some activities, there may be the additional challenge of pupils employing a technique that is effective in the short term, perhaps because the space or opposition allows it to be, but will cease to be so as performance level increases. In this situation it will be necessary to tweak the practice to allow a different movement solution to develop (chapter 7). Subject knowledge is critical here – think back to chapter 3 and how you might build your knowledge in those activities where you feel less confident. In your faculty, these most common errors could be highlighted in schemes of work to support colleagues and ultimately pupils.

Demonstrations

There are times when the best solution for everyone involved is for the teacher to demonstrate what is being learned. Because there's a lot of talk in life of people being either 'sporty' or 'not-sporty' this can sometimes be unhelpful. For example, a class of pupils who find PE harder may see a teacher who they have ascribed the 'sporty' label to proficiently showing a movement and think, 'Of course they can do it, they are a PE teacher.'

Here are some strategies that may help movements appear more accessible to pupils.

Become relatable: explain how hard you found it to learn a skill (not all the time, this would take too long). I commonly do this with basketball lay-ups. It's a skill that looks hard to start with, but is quite desirable for a lot of pupils, and looks a bit like basketball looks on TV (without the jump height!) I tell pupils that I didn't know what a lay up was until I learned to be a PE teacher. I learned how to do one at 25 years old, in my first year of teaching. (True story, thanks to my first head of department for teaching me!)

Use a pupil/pupils to demonstrate: This could be prepped in advance (chapter 5), or could be a live first-take. What is quite important here is to be mindful that always selecting a pupil/pupils to demonstrate who are already competent in the eyes of their peers is unlikely to remove the barriers felt by children who perceive themselves to be less competent. It's very tempting to use pupils to demonstrate who you know play a particular sport outside of school, or at a sports club, because you know/hope that the demonstration will be a good model for others. The social element of this is just as important here and builds belonging, so be thoughtful about who is involved and how.

Use examples and non-examples: In some demonstrations, it can be instructive to make some mistakes to highlight problems. I usually prep classes for this by saying: 'Sometimes I make accidental mistakes. Be sure to look out for these.' I'll then repeat the skill a few times, and in some of those repeats make the most likely/most problematic mistake. I'll make sure I don't only ask them what's happened after a mistake has been made. After at least one correct repeat I'll ask something like: 'You just watched me serve. What information can you give me?'

It is important that they will be able to tell their classmates why things are right, as well as why things are wrong. This Q&A sequence is extremely useful if you are expecting pupils to give feedback to each other. It gives the opportunity for them to see those most common errors we discussed earlier. You can also check that they can give suitable advice for correction, and positive feedback on why something was performed well.

NB: Sometimes it feels like it crushes pupils' dreams when they don't get to demo. There are some things that I will always choose to demo myself. However, in a 'spot the mistake' scenario, or where you just want to demo yourself, there's an easy way to involve a pupil, without taking thinking away from the rest of the class. Make a keen demo volunteer your 'coach' for the activity and prep the class and the coach that they will need to think hard about what to say to you after the demo(s). You can then cold call from the class, or the coach, or have one pupil answer and switch to another to check the answer by saying: 'What do you think about pupil 1s answer...(pause)... pupil 2? You can then make the point even clearer by getting the pupil coach to give the feedback to you directly, and trying to act on it in a subsequent demo.

Building complexity in small steps

In most situations our pupils are not yet experts. To manage their cognitive load we'll need to carefully share new information in smaller chunks than our passion and enthusiasm might drive us to. We can think back here to having clarity in exactly where we want pupils to get to, and the small steps that take them there. Splitting material into a series of shorter explanations, with practice time after each, is likely to be more effective (Rosenshine, 2012). In particular, this strategy supports the pupils that find learning harder – it ensures they are less likely to be left behind. It's also more likely that pupils will see success. Each step represents a smaller, more manageable challenge, motivating pupils to continue to try as the work gets harder.

The bigger picture

This is another 'curse of knowledge' situation. You are clear about why pupils need to learn this next thing. Maybe it is the logical next step in your sequence to improve their performances, or maybe it solves a problem they have. You might have even set up the contextual need, as highlighted in chapter 4. All of this is still much clearer to you than to the pupils. You have a well-developed overall picture that shows where and how it all fits together. It might feel like over-egging something, but it is necessary to narrate to pupils why this learning is useful. Making the 'value' explicit, and placing it firmly in the wider process of learning and improving can help pupils make the decision to give attention and effort (McCrea, 2020). Showing pupils how learning connects also helps them to organise their knowledge - relating one idea or skill to others they already know, or to how the skill operates in practice.

Making your explanation accessible

Take a moment to think about football commentary. Consider how many different ways the ball being played away from the centre of the pitch to the sidelines might be described.

You can probably come up with at least three or four:

'The ball has been played wide.'

'She's passed it to the winger.'

'Play has moved into the channel.'

'He's spread the play there; the width is stretching the defence.'

'That's good control, and now she drives down the line.'

In the situation where all the listeners are familiar with the sport or activity, using different terminology doesn't present too many problems. Unfortunately, this is rarely the case in our classrooms. Learners arrive with a wide range of prior knowledge and interest levels. Some will regularly play and watch a range of sports, others won't. Some will speak English at home, others are new to the language. Our expertise puts us at risk of reducing the clarity of our explanations, creating confusion, just as Bill Bryson is entertainingly baffled by cricket commentary in *Down Under: Travels In a Sunburned Country* (2000): 'I don't think I've seen offside medium slow fast pace bowling to match it since Baden-Powell took Rangachangabanga for a maiden ovary at Bangalore in 1948.'

In addition to having different terms for the same thing, we also have some high utility tier one and tier two words that have different meanings in different activities.

Drive:

In cricket, front foot, back foot, on, off.

To the basket in basketball

Shot in badminton; fast and flat.

Drive down the line (running in football/hockey, hitting a groundstroke in tennis).

Leg drive in rugby.

Riding a bike translates from some languages as driving a bike.

Shot in golf; long and high.

Knee/arm drive in sprinting.

With all of this in mind, we need to carefully use vocabulary in lessons in such a way that pupils are supported to build understanding. Initially, this will likely mean achieving consistency in which terms are used – departments should work together to identify their language of PE. In lessons, teachers can then explicitly teach what is meant, alongside examples and demonstrations. It's also important to bring to practical settings some of the strategies used regularly in traditional classrooms:

- Say the new word clearly, including tricky pronunciation.
- Pupils repeat the word back.
- Give pupils the chance to use the word in a sentence or discussion.
- Link the new word to other similar terms or words with the same stem.
- Show how the word is spelled (e.g. on a whiteboard).
- Revisit in later learning episodes – for example through Q&A to allow pupils regular retrieval opportunities.

Being clear about the vocabulary we're using, teaching new words, and moving learning forwards in small steps should all contribute to helping us build lean and efficient explanations where pupils' attention is directed to our intended outcomes.

Key takeaways

- Beware your own expertise. Try to think carefully about the knowledge pupils arrive at a situation with.
- Demonstrations are extremely helpful. Plan how these can be most effective in each lesson.

- Break learning down into small steps and keep explanations lean. This reduces the amount of new information pupils have to deal with at any one time and can help secure success for more pupils.
- Plan for how pupils will engage with explanations and demonstrations. Return to: how many pupils are thinking? How many are thinking hard?
- Explicitly teach new words and those that have a different meaning in PE.

CHAPTER 7
PRACTICE MAKES PROGRESS

There are two words I'll almost never say in PE. The first is 'unlucky' – most things in sport aren't unlucky, they just aren't quite good enough yet. Instead, I'll happily call out what did go well. For a shot that hits the bar, 'you did a great job to get something on that cross'. A two-point basket that doesn't get the drop, 'you shot high enough to give your teammate a good rebound'. The second word I avoid is 'perfect'. Not much is perfect and the idea that there is one 'perfect' way to perform a skill feels wrong anyway. How can there be one perfect cover drive in cricket when every ball and pitch and player is slightly different? Gary Player, a South African golfer is credited with the famous 'the more I practise, the luckier I get' quote. But it's not really luck, and as it's hard to say what perfection would even look like, I prefer to focus on the idea that practice makes progress. We might not get to perfect, but we can all get better.

Deciding how pupils will practise is a tricky business. In chapter 5, we looked at maximising practice time through controlling logistics, like cone set-ups and group numbers. In this chapter, we'll think more carefully about maximising practice outcomes through design and support.

Practice design

This is where we will enact those small steps in learning we spent time planning in chapter 4. Without a clear end point in mind, designing or selecting practice tasks becomes hard, so if you're stuck or unsure, return to the question: 'If this practice/lesson/unit is done well, what will it look like?'

There is also some strong research evidence to indicate how we might go about things. The barrier here is that there are some choices that are less likely to lead to long-term retention and transferability of learning, but in the short term, they improve the performance that is going on right in front of us. We also need to hit that 'Goldilocks' level of 'desirable difficulty' where it is hard enough to be an appealing challenge, but not so hard that it feels like too big a step (Bjork and Bjork, 2011). Here are some key considerations:

63

Variable practice is likely to lead to more success and stronger retention than blocked identical practice. In a bean bag throwing study, performance at throwing to a 3ft target was stronger in the group that had practised at 2ft and 4ft, as compared to a group who practised only at 3ft. These findings have been replicated in other sporting situations, including basketball shooting, where free throw distance shooting improved with practice from different distances (Soderstrom and Bjork, 2015). There are some other straightforward ways we can introduce variability, even in quite tightly controlled practices. Instead of having pupils in football stood at a cone, passing to another pupil stood at a cone, we can make sure that pupils make a positive movement in front of the cone to receive (straight or diagonally), or move back behind, varying the length and angle of each pass. This can probably be managed without the cone too – reducing the cone commitment.

Interleaved practice is better than repetitive practice for retention and transfer (Wright and Kim, 2019). The latter seems to be true both when taking a skill to a novel situation or when learning a novel task. This has interesting implications for us. Interleaving doesn't mean having a scattergun approach, randomly practising different skills in every lesson. It could mean that a lesson where serving in badminton is being practised involves serving to three different locations, as in one of the studies quoted previously. It could mean that although the main focus of a practice in volleyball is a new skill, spiking, there are opportunities in the lesson for pupils to recall and practice volley and dig.

The last chapter mentioned **simplifying, instead of isolating**. It's common to hear things like 'pupil n struggles to transfer skills to game situations'. We can help by using the ideas of representative learning design to make our practices look, feel, or play, like real-life game situations. A caveat here, not all mini-games or constraints-based practices are representative. 'Make sure everyone touches the ball before you score' might be seen to be inclusive, but in reality if I was on the wing with the ball and the striker was clean through with no defender I wouldn't be passing it back to the holding midfielder, so it is not representative of a game situation. By the same measure, it's possible to build practices that do play like the situation in a game, but aren't mini-games. We're aiming to create repetition, without exact repetition – lots of chances to practise the things that might happen, and what a suitable response might be, but not by closing off all other options and taking away decisions. To learn more about building constraints into practices, 'The Adaptable Coach' review article (Lindsay and Spittle, 2024) is a great starting point.

Designing game units

Coming up with tasks to solve problems that pupils are having is probably my favourite thing about being a teacher, both in practical and theory situations. Great tasks are what makes learning enactable for pupils. Chris McGrane (2020) summed it up in his book title when he described tasks as 'the bridge between teaching and learning'.

Harder or new sequences of movements or play often need to be practised in modified situations before pupils can be successful in full games. Rehearsing these small sections also helps to focus pupils' efforts on them as being important and gives a high number of practice opportunities. In game activities, I sometimes call these practices 'game units' for a few reasons:

- There's an immediate implication that what we are practising now will be useful in game situations.
- It sounds more fun than 'skills practice' or 'drill' because it has the word 'game' in.
- It keeps me focused on making sure this really replicates an in-game situation.

The following are some examples of problems and the 'game unit' practice that could solve them. Hopefully they also demonstrate some of the principles from the key considerations mentioned – variability, interleaving of skills, and practice that looks like the game.

Activity	Problem	Game unit practice/ progressions
Volleyball	Serve has been introduced, rallies are breaking down as first receive touch isn't effective.	Feeder on other side of net, player in setting position. Worker stands in back court and aims to pass feed to within 1 or 2 steps of setter, who catches it and sends it back under the net for next feed. The feed could be a throw, a self-fed volley, or eventually a serve from the back of the court. Progressions: If the pass from the worker is good, the setter can set the ball. A fourth player can move in to catch it. If the sets are good, the fourth player can spike. If the spikes are happening, the feeder or another player can block. At this point, we now have a three touch play on one side of the net and a game-like response on the other.
Badminton	Choosing between different overhead shots in the game.	Feeder shapes to throw, pauses and calls drop or clear. Two catchers are in position – one on the service line and one in the back tramlines on the opposite side of the net. Progressions: Catchers wait while sitting down/laying on fronts/ off court. During the pause, one catcher moves into position, there is now no verbal call. The worker hits the shot to the space on the court, i.e. not to the catcher. Group feeds back if correct decision has been made. Catchers get rackets and wait as previous. This time they are ready in a badminton ready position. If the shot is well-placed, they leave it. If it's within reach of them, they return it (as an attack if they can).

Activity	Problem	Game unit practice/ progressions
Football	Possession is being lost due to decision making in a game – time to turn or make a low-risk pass.	In threes, worker in the middle with a work area extending about 2 to 3m in front and behind. Two feeders are about 5m beyond this in each direction. As they send a feed in, they tell the worker whether there is 'time to turn' or 'player on'. In 'time to turn', the worker controls the ball, turns and sends it to the other feeder. In 'player on' they set it back to the player it came from, who has the forward view. Progressions: Worker meets the ball, moving to the edge of their work area to receive and recovering to the middle of it each time. In 'time to turn' the worker shapes to protect the ball and let it come across their body as they turn instead of control then turn. The waiting feeder can choose whether to stay in the feed position or run in to stand behind the worker – they become the stimulus for the call of 'player on,' when they are not there it's 'time to turn'.

Designing modified games

Earlier I mentioned a potentially unhelpful modification – the classic 'every player touches the ball'. It's possible to use modified rules, spaces, opponent numbers/actions, or equipment to manipulate players' decisions and increase the likelihood that they will find solutions in future games. Like many things in teaching, it's tempting to always be 'adding'. Consider the things you can strip out of modified games to provide a greater clarity of focus. For example, in touch rugby I might want players to be confident to try and attack space on their own, and maybe try to beat a defender one on one. I could implement a rule that you have to collect two touches before making a pass, and that you can still score after collecting the first touch. In this game, probably 4v4, what I'm hoping is that I will see players getting a lot of opportunity to run with the ball in hand, move into position to support teammates when they don't have the ball, and in defence, make quick movement towards the ball carrier to make the touches. For this reason, I would remove the sidelines in this game. I wouldn't use a never-ending try line that might really weight it towards the attackers. So the instruction would be, 'It doesn't matter how far wide to the sides you go in this game, but you can only score between the cones'. This means I don't need to worry about whether or not the players know how to get the ball back into play, the game will stop less often, and runs into space will be rewarded. Teams will still need to work out how to move the ball back into the scoring area if they go too wide, just like moving the ball away from going out of play in a full game.

I also really like naming the games that I will use again with a group – I find it helps make them memorable for pupils as it becomes a 'thing' and not just some practice they once did, you know, that day it rained. Chapter 5 mentioned how keeping the structure of practices the same can reduce the cognitive load for pupils – they don't have to learn the practice, just the slight difference to how we're doing it today as we try to learn something new. Here's a favourite game – the structure is repeatable and can be adapted, it's got a name, and it solves a problem players have.

Problem: In indoor cricket, you need to try to score off every ball that is not a wide/no ball. Running is particularly important as swapping places usually = 2 runs. Teams that don't hit walls with their shots or run poorly typically have low batting scores.

Game solution: 'A dot ball is not a hot ball.'

Played in half a sports hall, hitting away from the centre of the room. (Another game can happen in the other half, and there are a lot of wall hits.)

Players are split into two teams. Innings are timed or set number of balls. Batters **must** score every ball. Anyone who doesn't score (i.e. gets a dot) when they face a ball joins the back of the line (they will get another go) – it could have been the on strike or waiting batter who is culpable – the players can agree this. Batters retire at 12 and join the back of the line. Fielders can create dot balls by taking catches or effecting run outs and stumpings. The bowler is a feeder – underarm feed. They are allowed to target the stumps but should also give some that are outside the stumps on both sides.

What happens: This can be a slow starter – hesitant running, missed shots, etc. With more playing time, pupils realise that the reliable scores are side wall + run, or even defend, and run. The waiting batter must be really ready to go and clear communication is essential. It can also be useful for pupils to be run out and realise the runs that aren't actually there – it's really low stakes here if that happens and you will likely get another go later anyway.

Adaptations: This could also be used outside so long as the groups are small enough that there are spaces to hit into. I have also played the same game indoors but with the stumps right over to one side to practise hitting into the offside with a group of players that had started to play everything to leg side.

Supporting success

Success rate is crucial in pupil learning and there isn't a great difference between a success rate that is more likely to support learning and one that doesn't. Being successful or feeling like they have the agency to become so is also critical in creating and sustaining motivation. The challenge for us is that when pupils are novices in a sporting situation it can be very hard to achieve the 80–85% success rate suggested by Rosenshine (2012), or even the 70% indicated in sports skill acquisition research (Gray, 2022). There is also the complication that PE is very public by nature – pupils can easily compare theirs and others' performances, so managing support is even more important. We need pupils to remember feelings of success and satisfaction, not the moments they perceive that they got it wrong in front of their peers. For this reason, we will look at some of the ways we might tweak our practices to support pupils in achieving success more often.

Scaffolding by manipulating equipment

Scaffolding refers to anything we put in place to support pupils with new or particularly difficult tasks. This could be something physical, or a change to the task. There are a few obvious examples of the former from sport, like swimming noodles/woggles, or trampoline harnesses. There are also some other well-known ones that don't really help that much: armbands make it hard for new swimmers to achieve a flat body position, and stabiliser wheels on bikes can mean a new rider becomes dependent on leaning on them. Here are some common physical manipulations to tasks that can be highly effective in supporting pupil learning.

Changing the length of striking equipment

Striking tasks are some of the most challenging in PE in terms of the coordination, decision making and movement skills required. In general, the length of implements should relate to the height of the pupil. However, pupils who find it harder to coordinate striking tasks can be supported by offering a shorter racket/bat, or by being told to hold the existing one further up the handle. For some pupils, the latter can be a good option if it secures success without the pupil having to be seen by peers to have a different piece of equipment. Sometimes just holding a badminton racket a hand space up the grip can make a big difference, and it can be easier to 'remove' as a scaffold, as the length doesn't change much to move to the full length as the pupil improves.

Changing the weight of equipment

In an average athletics lesson, it probably doesn't matter if the discus, shot or javelin is the 'correct' weight for the age group. Those values are the correct competition weights. If you are preparing pupils to compete at external events, clearly these hold value. In PE lessons and school events, teachers should use their professional judgement to select the equipment that is the best fit for the pupils involved. Consider that which will best enable pupils to practise the desired techniques – only ever using very light shots for example might tempt pupils to 'throw' like an overarm throw, instead of 'pushing' as they will perceive the further distance gained with this technique to have been successful. The lightness means that there is no true need to use the correct form. Having a range of sizes of footballs, basketballs, rugby balls, and so on, is really helpful too.

The weight of striking equipment is also important; sticks, bats, and rackets should all be light enough for pupils to manipulate into different positions. For pupils moving to wooden cricket bats for example, it's worth investing in some lighter bats of smaller sizes, even though these may be more costly.

Changing other physical features

There are some movements and tasks that can be made easier (or harder) with other physical manipulations. Hoop height could be reduced in basketball and netball, or goal size changed in other invasion games. In gymnastics, it's possible to change the height of take-off and landing surfaces to suit the skill being learned. It can be a big help for pupils learning a forward roll to roll down a slope, by placing a mat over a take-off board for example. Front support can be made harder or easier by putting feet or hands on a raised surface respectively. Physical items can also be used to provide mechanical guidance to pupils as they practise. Examples include:

- In fencing, balancing bean bags on shoulders, in elbow crook, and/or on head to show balance in 'en garde' position or when practising footwork.
- In cricket, pupils sometimes hop in the bowling action. This is undesirable as it means the action is less controlled. Adding a low mini hurdle or similar into a slowed down version of the approach to the crease can support a pupil in developing the exaggerated step needed to get into their bowling action.
- In gymnastics, tucking a bean bag under the chin to maintain a good tuck position.
- In contact rugby, playing a mini game (could even be walking pace) with a swiss ball or other oversized ball. This means that the tackler must wrap the ball carrier low – the ball being carried is simply too big for anything else to happen!

As with any support, the key decisions then sit around how to remove the help such that pupils can continue to progress. In some cases, such as the lighter bat, there's no need to – unless the pupil is aiming to play hardball school or club cricket, the plastic bat will serve their purpose adequately.

Scaffolding by supporting decision making

Giving visual or verbal cues in earlier stages of learning can really support pupils in applying skills in decision making situations. Given that we are ultimately aiming for pupils to be able to select and apply skills fluently and effectively, this is of great benefit. Here's an example of identifying line as a batter (deciding which balls to attack, and which to defend) in cricket.

Recap aims of batting in cricket:

- Score runs.
- Stay in. You can't score runs from the pavilion.

The class have previously practised the front foot drive in various scenarios, including mini games. Some players were clean bowled, playing attacking shots at straight balls. To move play forward, a defensive shot is needed for straight balls that would go on to hit the stumps. Pupils are in groups of four with a set of stumps, one bat, and a number of balls as appropriate to the class (six per group; one per group on a Friday afternoon at full moon in a strong wind). Tennis balls or windballs will both be fine for this.

The warm-up could consist of practising front foot drives with this set up, or the first activity here would work as the starter.

A clear demonstration and teaching points are given for the front foot defence, including advice for the feeder.

Step 1: In the first round of the practice, the feeder sends the batter balls that are aimed at the stumps using a bobble feed. A wicket keeper is ready for missed balls/poor feeds and a 'coach' is to the side checking the stance and step. There is no decision to make, a front foot defence is played to each ball, though there will be some variance from the feed – this won't be exactly the same flight/bounce/line every time. Feedback could take the form of the feeder telling the batter whether their bat is more vertical or horizontal – this may have happened in previous practising of drives.

Step 2: If the batter is making regular contact with the ball, in the next set of feeds, they can vary between some feeds that are on the stumps, and some that are off target. For ball/player circulation, it's easier if this is done to the same side for all groups, i.e. all off targets to the off-side or all to the leg side. (I would always choose offside here, most players are much happier playing to leg side.) Critically, the feeder will tell the batter as they release the ball whether it is on target 'defend' or off target, could use 'attack' or 'drive.' So, the batter now has two different skills to employ, but they are being told each time which to use. The 'coach' can become a more active fielder. The feeder can say whether the correct shot was selected.

> Where could this go wrong?
>
> **Feeds aren't matched to verbal cue.** Help this by using existing lines and putting a middle stump on a line. Most feeders will be able to send the ball along a straight line from around 5–8m away. Could check the feed quality in advance by having a warm-up game that involves underarm throws at the stumps or to a keeper.

Step 3: Same feeds, no verbal cues. Now the batter must select from the two shots without a cue. They should still receive instant feedback from the feeder about whether they chose correctly. At any point, it's easy to put back in the verbal cues with no big drama or public embarrassment for the pupil if needed.

Step 4: Mini game. Feeders instead of bowlers – directed to mix up between on the stumps feeds and those that are not on target. There should only be 1–2 on the stumps feeds in each over. Feeders vs bowlers here is quite a useful distinction, it removes the idea that the 'bowler' is attacking the batter. Instead we're constructing a situation where the feeder *could* get a clean bowled wicket, but what we are actually hoping is that the straight balls are defended, and the others are driven, giving the fielding team plenty to collect. Teacher/TA could feed in one of the mini games and give verbal cues as needed.

Thinking back over the material in this chapter we can highlight several benefits to this kind of practice sequence:

- Still a relatively high volume of repetition – groups of 3 or 4 means lots of turns.
- There is variability to the practice straight away because there is no 'tee' activity. The bobble feed is relatively easy to hit from a good stance but will be slightly different each time to allow the movement skill to develop.
- Learning is supported by visual and verbal information that can be removed/re-added as required. Decision making still happens early in the process, not just in the game at the end.
- The practice set up immediately had the shape of the game; this feels like cricket.
- The planned sequence takes us to a mini game. Pupils often look forward to this part of the learning; playing games with your friends is fun – remember our quote from chapter 2!

Another way to support pupils in their decision making is by giving them longer to make the decision. This can be done in a few ways:

- Reduce the pace of play, e.g. by playing walking rugby. This can help players practice deciding when to tackle, as they can better organise getting their feet and body in the right place/shape.
- Increase the space available, e.g. in a 4v2 keep-away game in netball or football, which will give the attacking team (4) longer on the ball.

- Give an additional task to the opposition. For example, in touch rugby, when a touch is made, all defenders must touch their own try line or touch their chest to the floor. In net sports, the projectile could be caught on the other side of the net and then fed to give a player longer to get into a position before they must respond to the next challenge.

Key takeaways

- Practice tasks are key to learning. Applying variation to practices and interleaving instead of blocking practice are both good bets. Be aware that this might mean initial performances look less good, but longer-term retention and transfer are likely to be better.
- Try to design practices that are as representative as possible of real-life scenarios. This doesn't mean everything has to be a game, but including the decision-making aspects early in the process is key.
- Modifying games doesn't always mean adding rules/constraints. Consider what you can take away to reduce load and focus learning.
- Instead of reducing the task even further when pupils struggle, consider what scaffolds you can put in place to support them. This could include changing the equipment, cues, speed or space.
- Consider the importance of routines and similar structures in being time and load efficient (chapter 5). How can the practices you select or design contain repeatable but adaptable elements?

CHAPTER 8
CLASSROOM DIALOGUE

A silent practical PE lesson would be unusual. In many activities, pupils need to communicate verbally to work together successfully. They may need to call for the ball, organise who is marking who, or remind a classmate of a rule or idea. Well-designed classroom talk can really enhance the participation ratio ('how many pupils are thinking?') and the think ratio ('how hard are pupils thinking?') in the lesson (see *Teach Like a Champion*, 2021 for more on ratio). There are several ways we can add this kind of talk to lessons however, in a practical setting there's the tension that during the time we ask pupils to engage in structured talk and listening they are not active. This means that we need to carefully balance talk tasks, which allow the gathering of useful formative information, with lesson design that allows for a high proportion of active time.

Questioning

Planning questioning episodes in advance is vital in maximising practical work time in lessons. In chapter 5, questions to check for task understanding were discussed. This section concentrates on checking the knowledge that pupils have understood, though many of the same strategies apply.

Building high-quality questions

Sometimes questions are used for quick checks. Mini whiteboards are great for these kinds of questions, and I can use a routine to sample responses quickly and effectively. In practical PE, I might use cold call (more on this later). All the pupils are thinking, but these aren't always the questions that get the really hard thinking going. For that, I need to ask more in-depth, open questions. This is much harder.

The biggest clue that a question could have been better is when you have to say 'That's a correct answer, but it's not what I'm looking for'. When planning questions, we can refer back to the question: 'If this goes well, what does good look like?' If the question is such that everyone can give some response, and it's also possible for pupils to give a strong, extended

75

answer then the question was likely well-designed. In my current PE faculty this is something we practise together – taking questions and refining them for use in lessons. Here are some principles we try to apply:

- Keep questions open not closed. Yes or no alone shouldn't be available as answers.
- Overlong questions can be confusing/unfocused. It's not a hard rule but try to rephrase questions that are longer than 12 words.
- Using words like 'could', 'all', and 'even' to promote depth of response.

Here are a set of questions we recently practised upgrading:

Q: Which barrier to participation could affect a teenager?

Upgrade option 1: What are all the barriers to participation that could affect a teenager?

With this upgrade, pupils are prompted to think of multiple barriers. In the original question, they can think of one then switch off.

Upgrade option 2: Which barrier to participation could most affect a teenager?

Pupils still need to think of multiple barriers here to identify the one with the biggest impact. We probably get slightly less in volume here, but a bit more in terms of evaluating. There is also the option to follow up an answer with 'What other barriers could you have considered?' or 'Which barriers could affect a teenager even more?'

Q: Your opponent has served low in badminton, what do you do?

Upgrade option 1: Your opponent has served low in badminton, what are all your options?

Again, this pushes for multiple options.

Upgrade option 2: Your opponent has served low in badminton, what could *your* best option be?

This retains the need to consider multiple options, but also themselves as a player. Pupil answers could be different here, especially as they become more expert, and that would probably be a good thing.

Here are the rest of the set of questions, try upgrading them yourself:

- Can you give me a rule for serving in badminton?
- How can you be out in cricket?

- Which media type would be useful to your local club?

Strategies for asking questions

There are many places to read about high leverage questioning strategies; consider Doug Lemov's *Teach Like a Champion 3.0* (2021) and *The Coaches Guide to Teaching* (2020), or Tom Sherrington's *Rosenshine's Principles in Action* (2019) for a more succinct overview.

Let's take a closer look at using different questioning strategies in practical PE lessons.

Strategy	Overview	PE considerations
Cold call	Pose the question, give silent thinking time, name the pupil, collect the response.	It can be tempting to rush the thinking time to get back to practical work. If you have decided the question is important, the thinking time is too, so make sure you give enough.
		For the same reason, avoid only taking one sample answer. Collecting a wider sample ensures that you can be more responsive to the level of understanding in the class. It also means that pupils engage in the process. If you consistently only ask one pupil their answer, it can be very tempting to not bother to think – the odds are in your favour at 1/28ish.
		In *Tips for Teachers* (2022), Craig Barton details some ways to improve cold call. These are my two favourite ways to really 'supercharge' your cold call routine.
		- Wait for a moment before you respond to the pupil answers. This means that other pupils can think about the answer they heard and haven't switched off from the sequence because you have praised it (therefore thinking is over).
		- After the wait, still don't tell the class what you think about the answer... yet. Thank the pupil and keep the jeopardy going – ask the class what they think about what they have heard or collect another response to compare.

Strategy	Overview	PE considerations
Think, pair, share	Pose the question, give thinking time. Give partner talk time. Collect responses.	This can be a great bridge to cold call, if you are worried a class/some pupils might find it intimidating to be called upon. You could circulate during 'pair' and build confidence for pupils who struggle with contributing in front of peers by saying, 'You're having a great conversation here; I'd like your classmates to hear it, so I'll make it look like a surprise, but I'll be asking you in a moment.' The risk for the more nervous pupil is removed as they already know their response is a good one. You haven't had to (publicly) break any routines.
Say it again, better	When a student gives a part response, or uses informal language, ask them to say it again, better.	This is really helpful in PE, both in practical and theory lessons. In PE some of the formality of lessons has been removed – we're outside, wearing trainers! This means that some pupils 'forget' that they need to use formal, correct language when answering questions. This can carry over into their exam PE courses. For this reason, it's a good idea to build good habits in Key Stage 3, and challenge pupils to reword or upgrade their answers.

Classroom talk

In this section we are concerned with planned talk between pupils during non-active parts of practical lessons and in theory lessons. Where this is effectively deployed, there are a range of benefits. Well-structured classroom talk:

- can help pupils make sense of challenging concepts.
- offers a bridge between hearing about or seeing an idea/concept and being expected to write about it or replicate it practically.
- provides a lower risk space for pupils to try out answers before answering in front of peers.
- allows the teacher to collect data about where pupils are at with their thinking.

- gives opportunities for new or specialist language to be spoken aloud in context and on multiple occasions.
- is interesting and engaging.
- can be academically rigorous.

Structuring classroom talk

There are three main things we need to consider to maximise the effectiveness of talk episodes:

- Who talks to who, and any other logistical routines.
- How the talk is structured.
- How the responses are collected.

Who talks to who

In chapter 5, the importance of routines was established and examined. Having a consistent routine for pupil talk in lessons can help to ensure that learning time is maximised. For theory lessons, carefully consider the seating plan, such that pupils have a talk partner that supports/challenges them as appropriate. For example, it may be helpful to seat an EAL pupil with a more fluent (in English) partner who speaks the same home language. In practical lessons, being clear about the organisation of this when there are no desks to sit behind is still important. Talking in pairs rather than larger groups gives more pupils the opportunity to talk and makes it more likely that they will be an active listener in the partnership. In a larger group, the social pressure to listen is slightly lessened – there's someone else there that might do it.

How the talk is structured

Ensure that it is clear to pupils what they are supposed to be talking about. You could use 'check for task understanding' questions before saying 'go' on the talk task. Keeping a consistent approach to the types of talk task also helps – it's like having a routine within a routine. Here's the three types of talk task I use most regularly in PE lessons.

Talk task	What's this all about?	Practical example	Theory example
Answer and justify	Identifying a correct, preferred or ideal technique or strategy, either from a MCQ, list, or their memory. Pupils then need to explain their choice.	Explain which defensive strategy your team will employ.	Which type of media would you use to promote a sports club aimed at 16–19 year olds? Explain your answer.
Ranking/ ordering	Pupils ranking ideas/concepts or identifying relative importance.	*(Three hoops are set up in a badminton service box).* Which of these three areas would you be most likely to serve to? Why?	A footballer is aiming to improve their CV endurance. Rank these training types from most effective (1) to least effective (3): Continuous training Interval training Circuit training
Recalling	Pupils recalling previously studied ideas.	Partner A tell partner B everything you can remember about defending in netball. Partner B, listen carefully. When your teammate has finished you can add extra details or correct them if needed.	Partner A will point at a joint. Partner B will identify the bones and muscles sited there. They can extend by adding joint actions and antagonistic pairs. Partner A could have a textbook to check the information. Then swap.

In the classroom there are usually more opportunities to scaffold talk than in a practical situation. Outdoors, you could support pupils by giving individual thinking time in advance of the discussion. Verbally giving scripts or sentence starters is likely to be problematic, as pupils will need to hold that information in their heads whilst also thinking about your (hopefully challenging) question/task. Here's how you might provide a tight structure to discussions in theory or indoor lessons, where you have a whiteboard, screen, or handout available.

Question: What type of training would you recommend for a 15-year-old tennis player?

Think carefully about your answer.

Now that you have thought about your reasons, you're going to talk with your partner. Listen to them carefully.

If your partner says something you think is incorrect, at the end of their explanation you will have a chance to give your ideas. Use this script to help you.

Partner 1:

'I would recommend _____ training for a tennis player because...'

Partner 2:

'I agree, because in the sport of tennis players need to...'

Or

'I agree/disagree, and I recommend _____ training because...'

Collecting responses

Creating certainty around response collection is crucial to the effectiveness of talk tasks – not only will pupils be asked to provide a response, but responses are also valued and important to the learning process.

Here are some suggestions for building that culture and for collecting quality data.

Avoid	Instead
Using a talk task as a filler while you, for example, set up a visualiser, especially whilst you are embedding a routine.	Circulate while pupils talk, listening to conversations.
Only cold calling one pupil/pair after a talk task.	Take a wider sample. Use a super-charged cold-call technique from earlier in the chapter.

Avoid	Instead
Asking pupils to write a lot on their MWB and then display it. You might find it hard to see clearly a weight of thinking. Or problem areas.	Use MWB for a ranking task, for example, and ask pupils to write the top factor/idea on the MWB. You can then ask some pupils to share their reasons.
Letting talk tasks overrun.	Use a timer to maintain a sense of urgency around learning.

Sometimes teachers worry about pupil talk episodes, especially with more challenging or less engaged classes. There is perhaps the feeling of a slight loss of control, or that talk might not be a good use of time if it doesn't go well. Having a plan and routines in place can reduce this risk.

Here are some possible solutions to the most common worries.

Problem	Possible solution(s)
1. What if pupils don't talk about what I have asked them to talk about?	• Ensure that in giving instructions for the task, the rationale/follow-up task is identified. 'You will be talking to your partner about issue *y* so that you can answer a follow up question from me/so that you will be even more ready to write up your thoughts or answer some written questions.' • Narrate the positive: 'Thank you for your contributions. I have heard so many excellent in-depth conversations about this.' Make it seem like the social norm here is to be on task. • If it's just one or two pairs, visit them and say something like this: 'I know you haven't been doing this task. You have been talking about x or y. I'm not going to ask you the question in a moment because I don't want to embarrass you or put you on the spot in front of your friends. You will need to listen especially carefully to the answers though, as you missed the talk time. You must be ready to answer a question later in the lesson.' Then make sure you ask them one!
2. What if the talk quality is low?	• Reflect on the initial input: did you give pupils enough information? Had links to previous learning been made explicit? Were pupils 'primed' for this talk? • Was additional support needed prior to or during the discussion?

Problem	Possible solution(s)
3. Classroom talk is taking too long/ class doesn't settle/ similar concern.	• Practice the routines. Ensure that the method of participation in response collection is clear so that a purposeful individual (and therefore quiet) action follows the talk or response collection. • Use it more sparingly until the routine is clear. • Check out *Teach Like a Champion* (2021) – Brighten the Lines. • Keep to the time; consider a visible timer.

Peer coaching and feedback

This type of classroom dialogue probably has the biggest chance of variability in terms of effectiveness but could be really high leverage because pupils can watch their classmates for 100% of turns in a practical activity. Assuming that they attempt an equal distribution, teachers might see 3 or 4% of each pupils' practice. Pupils being able to give precise and helpful information to each other would significantly increase the quantity of feedback each individual pupil receives in the lesson. The challenge is to ensure that the quality is retained.

In a worst-case scenario, a pupil could receive a high quantity of unhelpful feedback that hinders their progress rather than accelerating it. This means we must select carefully which elements of a practice or game pupils will give feedback on. The more novice the class is, the more we must make what they are looking for clear and easily identifiable. It is also essential to train classes in how to give feedback and how to receive it. Handily, novices do seem to benefit from peer feedback in PE (Johnson & Ward, 2001), so this effort could be well placed. Intuitively, it feels like the more complex the skills performances and the more expert the performer, the harder it is likely to be for peers to accurately analyse what is going on and provide helpful feedback. Getting pupils into good habits with this early in learning could be very helpful.

How do you choose what exactly pupils should give feedback on? Identify black/white or yes/no binary situations. Sometimes these might relate to rules such as the server having their foot behind the service line in badminton, or a free-throw taker not crossing the line before the ball goes through the hoop in basketball. In other situations, they may be technique related, such as the bowler having a straight elbow in cricket, or a gymnast having their chin on their chest in a forward roll. Tactical ideas could also be checked, for example a badminton player stepping forward after sending a short serve.

Case study

Peer feedback opportunities in cricket bowling

Aspect of performance	Ease for pupils to ID	Suggested feedback	Potential impact
Grip: finger position could be variable but ball shouldn't be in palm.	Easy: can get performer to show them how they are holding it.	Hold the ball with the flat of your fingers. (Strokes own to show.)	High: bowling with ball in palm is hard!
Straight elbow so as not to throw.	Easy, if shown demo.	Tell your friend if their elbow was straight, or not straight.	High: makes bowling action correct and look to pupils like a real cricket bowl.
Arm passes next to ear on way to release point.	Easy, if shown demo.	Tell them there was a gap. Show your friend your arm passing next to your ear. Remind them to reach up tall.	High: increase accuracy of bowling.
Front arm is not showing bowling arm the way.	Medium: pupils with more experience can usually watch for this.	Remind your friend to slice down the batter with their front arm.	High: increase accuracy of bowling.
Front foot is past the crease	Easy but not worth worrying about earlier in learning.	Yes No, it's a no ball. Second time 'Check your run up working back from the crease.'	Medium: may have been a one ball error. Pupil may not be able to pace out run up correctly.

Aspect of performance	Ease for pupils to ID	Suggested feedback	Potential impact
Ball is wide	Easy, if lines are put in and pupil giving feedback is in the umpire's position.	Wide/not wide.	Low: this is knowledge of outcome, not performance. Even more experienced pupils may not be able to ID why the ball went wide that time.

How pupils talk to each other will be important in how impactful peer feedback is. Unfortunately, some of the role models that pupils see in some sports outside of school don't always speak respectfully. As the teacher you can build the culture of how pupils speak to each other. Sometimes with younger classes I ask pupils to give each other 'kind reminders' of rules. You can also narrate to them how important their role is in helping their friends learn. This helps to keep things learning focused, not mistake-focused.

Teacher feedback

Here we will deal with some of the dialogue that happens during lessons in response to pupil work – both theory and practical.

Firstly, a note on not talking. Sometimes practices aren't going that well and it can be tempting to intervene early doors. Often this isn't needed (assuming a good practice has been selected). It just takes multiple reps to get going with the practice. This is especially true when pupils are learning a new skill and a new practice. Take a moment to step back and fully scan what is going on:

Maybe those two pupils aren't chatting, they are just checking in on what happens next. Maybe it's ok that the first two reps from the far group were a bit slow, the pace is a bit faster on the third and fourth.

Maybe there is a common problem across all groups, even after a few practice turns, and the whole class needs additional instruction, in which case, you are in a better position to intervene in an informed way because you collected more 'data' by watching for just a little longer.

I suspect that it is more tempting to jump in straight away with activities where you feel less confident in your teaching – I find I'm more tempted to do this in fencing which I have only taught for a couple of years. The difficulty probably also exists in areas of high-expertise, where you know loads of tweaks (more on this later). Unless it is unsafe for some reason, try to avoid intervening before things have a proper chance to get going.

Keeping focus

Now that you have scanned the practice or theory task fully and find that it is underway in a way you are happy with, it's time to look more closely at the work. For best effect, this is an active process of observation. You are looking to see if pupils are trying to implement your instructions, and to what extent they are successful. It is highly possible that sometimes you can look at what is going on without really 'seeing' it (Lemov, 2020). Also bear in mind that as a relative expert and likely enthusiast, you may spot lots of things that you could give pupils advice on. To give effective and actionable feedback, we need to look at learning through the lens of our intended outcomes. That's not to say we can't warmly praise when other lovely things happen, like a kind moment, or a brilliant side-step, or a really good example in a paragraph. Our feedback however needs to be much more focused and considered.

Imagine for a moment that you are watching some Year 11 GCSE PE pupils playing volleyball. It's a pretty good game, both teams are attempting to use three touches and using legal shots. It's likely still the case that with every single point you could find something to highlight in the play:

'Great serve Monik, I saw you look for the space on the court!'

'Super calling everyone!'

'Strong jump there Miriam, next snap your wrist to speed up the shot.'

'Remember, when receiving serve, the player at 6 is behind their teammates so they have a clear view.'

All of these are legitimate things I could say to the pupils. But in a matter of minutes, I have referred to multiple aspects of play. If I am a player in this game, what should I be concentrating on here? Sometimes the immediacy of feedback gives it really high value. I find this to be especially the case if there is something a player is struggling with and they finally manage it. To me, that situation feels worth recognising immediately. There's also a risk that if I leave it too long, then try to respond to something that happened, the pupils won't remember quite what it was or what it looked like. The feedback won't have clarity or hold value. We don't want to keep stopping pupils all the time though, so there's a real need to be a teacher and not a commentator. This holds true in theory classrooms too – sometimes pupils need time to work through things without additional information. A constant narration can be distracting.

Here is some general advice:

- Think carefully before you pause the activity and be sure about what it is you really want to communicate. Is this relevant to everyone, or is this an individual feedback opportunity?
- Sometimes an immediate freeze to show exactly what's happened is really useful. You can make this a routine so that it happens quickly, feedback is given, and activity is resumed with minimal fuss.
- Be punchy in the delivery – precision not expansion.
- If possible, show pupils what you mean with a demonstration.
- Use already familiar terms or actions where possible.
- Avoid repeating yourself; if you're not sure if pupils have understood, ask questions.
- Make sure there is an action that pupils can take as a direct response to your intervention.
- Remember the feedback should be more work for them than for you, e.g. if you are live marking, instead of adding ticks/error marks, you could say: 'There are three mistakes in your list/answer/table. Try to find and correct them.'
- Avoid too much general praise: 'great shot' or 'good pass', for example. It is a far better idea to add *why* it was good: 'Great pass – I saw you look for the player in space.'

A note on assessment in PE

In core PE, there are a lot of opportunities to watch pupils and see where they are at and where they need to go next. This type of assessment directly informs my next steps in teaching. What is often much harder in PE is where there is a requirement to quantify this or record it in some more formal way. If how this is done needs to align with school-wide procedures, this adds an additional layer of complexity. A number of PE-specific models are available, such as Head, Hands, Heart (YST, 2019).

Having clarity around curriculum and unit aims here is essential – if you're not sure where you're going, it's hard to know how far you've got.

In examination courses, think carefully about the design and scheduling of key tasks or tests that help prepare pupils for coursework submissions or terminal examinations, as well as informing your next steps in teaching.

Key takeaways

- Routines can make classroom dialogue more effective by removing load from pupils and speeding up the pauses in activity.
- Great questions allow for a range of response depths.
- Have a clear plan for how responses will be collected. This helps to keep accountability on pupils and gives the teacher good quality information to make decisions about the next learning steps.
- Don't be a commentator. Look closely at what is happening in practical tasks and give clarity to your feedback with precise explanations and practical demonstrations.

CHAPTER 9
TEACHING THEORY PE

There are a range of courses available in the UK for pupils who are 14 to 16 years of age (usually level 2/GCSE equivalents), and in the post-16 sector (pupils who are attending sixth form or further education colleges). GCSE and A-level courses in PE usually consist of an internally assessed practical portion, a written coursework assignments, and two examination papers. Courses labelled as 'vocational' include a smaller weighting to the exam component, they are less practical and involve more written coursework. The content of the latter is usually more focused with courses named 'sports studies' containing more sociological content compared to 'sports science' courses which consist mainly of physiology. The content of GCSE and A-level PE often reflects a hybrid of these, combining physiology, biomechanics, psychology and sociology of sport. It could be argued that these qualifications are currently more 'sports science' than 'PE'. For departments choosing which qualification(s) to offer, there are a range of issues and factors to consider. Many of these are likely to be context specific. The next sections examine some key factors in delivering 14+ examination courses in PE with a particular focus on 14-16 Level Two qualifications.

Task selection and design

In chapters 5 and 7 we looked in detail at tasks in practical lessons from structural and pedagogical viewpoints. Much of the same advice holds true here.

- Repeating task formats reduces cognitive load for pupils; they don't have to learn the task and learn the material.
- Tasks should become increasingly difficult in small steps.
- Consider how scaffolds can be added or removed to support and challenge pupils as needed.
- Check for task understanding rigorously before work starts – everyone feels better about this than having to stop and have something re-explained.

Much of the research into classroom task structure comes from maths. I find McGrane's (2020) streamlining of earlier work into classifying tasks really helpful. He identifies three broad levels of type, increasing in difficulty. The following table below how this might be adapted for theory PE.

Type	Example activities	What might this look like in PE?
Procedural fluency	Developing fluency with identifying components. Recall quizzing Short answer questions	Naming bones, muscles, joints actions, user groups, media types MWB activities, paired or self-quizzing Practising 1 and 2 mark AO1 exam questions
Conceptual understanding	Sorting and matching, categorising Identifying/discussing relative importance Multiple representations	List provided – sort into bones, muscles or neither Ranking tasks, like the examples in chapter 8 Comparing/contrasting ideas or information Recognising ideas in a new situation, e.g. an example from a different sports action in movement analysis Being able to generate own examples
Problem solving	Hypothesising Evaluating	Applying knowledge: To make predictions in discussions. 'Explain what could be the most effective ways to increase women's participation in Leicester'. To evaluate or discuss concepts in demanding exam questions.

High value tasks

It's worth developing your own 'bank' of material placed in the task structures you intend to repeat. You can then tweak the exact content to suit your classes. These are 'high value' because you have decided to make them so – they can be replicated for different content and can be adapted easily for challenge and support.

Here are three structures I use regularly.

1. Table sorting

Using a quick two or three column table, I display a list of components on the board and ask pupils to sort them into the correct column. This would often be a recall starter task.

Pupils need to be able to do this task without spending time drawing out the table, so I would prep the table beforehand for them to ensure they can settle straight into doing the task.

For the answers in neither, add what they could be classified as.

Bone	Muscle	Neither

Hip flexors	Clavicle
Scapula	Femur
Thigh	Talus
Deltoid	Humerus
Thumb	Knee
Pectorals	Biceps
Tibia	Patella
Elbow	Shoulder
Gluteals	Cranium
Sternum	Hamstring
Wrist	Pelvis

Make it easier: At the start, fill in a couple while modelling thinking.

Make it harder: Ask pupils to explain one choice for each column underneath.

After a few minutes, show your own version under the visualiser, which has a couple of deliberate mistakes, and ask pupils to find them

2. Table gap fill

I love how tables can organise and connect knowledge.

Sporting action	Joint and movement	Agonist and contraction type	Antagonist	Plane	Axis
Squat, downward phase	Knee	Quadricep eccentric			
Cricket front foot drive	Elbow				
Tennis forehand	Shoulder internal rotation	Pectoral concentric	Deltoid		
Basketball take off for jump shot	Ankle				
Netball interception	Shoulder abduction				
Bicep curl					

Athlete	Intake	Expenditure	Energy balance	Outcome
A	2000kcal	3000kcal	-1000kcal Negative energy balance	
B	8000kcal		In energy balance	
C	4500kcal	4000kcal		
D	1000kcal	3000kcal		
E		3000kcal	+1200kcal Positive energy balance	
F				This athlete's body mass is likely to remain stable

Make it easier: Careful modelling sequence (I do); longer handover with Q&A (we do).

Make it harder: Fewer pre-completed cells. Entire blank rows for pupils to generate their own examples.

3. Tick, Trash, Improve

This is another maths steal (thanks Craig Barton, 2017).

The great thing about this is that I can start to make clear to pupils what is needed to secure exam marks. It's possible to write things that are factually correct but are not sufficiently detailed or applied to get exam marks. These are the 'improve' category.

Statement	Tick, trash, improve	Justify/refine
Alveoli are small and shaped like bunches of grapes. Their number and shape means that there is a large surface area available for diffusion in the lungs.	TICK	*Here, I justify why I have 'ticked' the statement. I also give additional details to practise using my knowledge.* The structure of alveoli is accurately described. The structure is then related to function as they are the site of gas exchange in the lungs. Alveoli are surrounded by a dense network of capillaries.
There is a higher concentration of CO_2 in the alveoli than in the blood. CO_2 diffuses from the alveoli into the bloodstream.	TRASH	*Here, explain why this is wrong or write a correct version.*
There is more oxygen in the alveoli than in the blood.	IMPROVE	*This is not clear or accurate enough. Use your knowledge to upgrade this statement.*
The only muscles involved in breathing are the diaphragm and the intercostal muscles.		

Statement	Tick, trash, improve	Justify/refine
Air can never be completely expelled from the lungs. The amount that remains in the lugs at all times is called the residual volume.		
Tidal volume changes when exercising.		
Deoxygenated blood arrives back at the lungs from the working muscles. Here, it diffuses into the alveoli to be exhaled.		

Statement	Tick, trash, improve	Justify/refine
A wall toss test is completed with a tennis ball. The participant stands 2m away from a wall. They throw the ball at the wall with one hand and catch it with the other hand, aiming for as many repetitions as possible in 30 seconds.	TICK	
The bleep test shows how fast participants can run 20 metre shuttles.	TRASH	
In the Illinois agility test, participants have to change direction at speed.	IMPROVE	

Statement	Tick, trash, improve	Justify/refine
A footballer could improve their power for jumping for a header using a vertical jump test.		
Agility is important to a basketball player, as during the game they will need to change direction as possession changes from one team to the other. Doing this quickly could allow them to beat an opponent to the ball.		
Coordination is important to a batter in cricket, as they need to be able to time the movement of their hands so that the bat hits the ball bowled at them.	IMPROVE	
Cardiovascular fitness is the most important component of fitness for a footballer.		

Make it easier: Give more examples. Remove 'improve' to start with and just go for tick/trash.

Make it harder: Give less guidance once fluent. Include the most common mistakes. There's an element of differentiation by outcome here as pupils re-write the improve/trash answers.

Practical tasks in theory lessons

There are some activities that pupils can physically do to enhance learning. These hands-on tasks can provide memorable concrete examples to support pupils' understanding and their ability to apply knowledge to practical sporting situations – a key assessment objective of most examination courses. The key thing for teachers is to ensure that these are planned in such a way that there is a precise and firm focus on the area of study and distractions are limited. Some specification content suits this well, for example, change in heart rate with exercise, movement analysis, and classification of skills. In some situations, practicals could be done up front, to give real-life examples and experiences for pupils to later 'stick' their theoretical knowledge to. I think it's much easier to learn about plyometric training by first *doing* a training session. In other topics, hands-on activities could allow pupils to recall, test and show previously learned knowledge.

Hands-on example: Skill classification

Pupils had previously been introduced to the topic and had placed some well-known sports skills on classification continua.

Pupils were given an adjustable table tennis net, some plastic cups and table tennis balls. They had a two-person desk available as a playing surface.

In groups of three or four, pupils were instructed to design some kind of quick game. The game had to be simple to play, with a way of discerning a winner.

The pupils were then challenged to adapt their game based on the skill classification continua. For example, they were asked to modify rules to make it:

- more self-paced.
- more closed.
- more fine/precise in terms of movement.

Some games were shown to the rest of the class for discussion. There was plenty of opportunity for questioning in the working groups, and with the whole class. For example:

- 'Which of these two games includes the most open skills?'
- 'What makes this game more externally paced than the other?'

Explaining and modelling

I realised a few years ago that while cycling to and from school, I spend a reasonable amount of ride time practising explanations in my head.

Rehearsing explanations can be really helpful in making them leaner. It's even better if you can do this with a colleague or record yourself (start with audio if you find watching yourself back too hard). Think through in advance what questions pupils might have or where they could get 'stuck'. Chapter 6 outlined some ways of practising new vocabulary to help pupils. In classroom lessons, we have a few additional options in the form of word maps, Frayer models, or word ladders. Pre-teaching new vocabulary can help pupils make sense of explanations. Giving multiple concrete examples is also helpful. Here we benefit from things in PE being generally very tangible – sponsors' logos are very visible in sport on TV, sports movements can be actioned or seen. With the latter we can again bring gesture and movement into learning by asking pupils to plantar flex their foot while we describe it or even place their hands on their ribs while talking about breathing. Pupils should also be asked to trace diagrams with their fingers during teacher or peer explanations, for example the pathway of blood through the heart, and initially shown how to do this (Turner, Goodwin and Caviglioli, 2022).

Modelling written tasks

There is a slight strangeness to PE teaching in that the outcomes of your exam groups have high accountability, yet it's likely you will only spend 10–15% of your teaching time delivering in a theory classroom. You get a lot less practice at it; there might be only two or three lessons per week where you use a visualiser versus an English teacher's 20. I'll repeat from earlier: rehearse with a colleague or video recording for feedback. The PE teachers I know who are really effective with their exam classes are master modellers and also promote strong metacognitive strategies for their pupils.

- They know the specification and assessment objectives inside out and have used examiners' reports to identify common problems in pupil responses.
- They start slowly and engage pupils in the process by asking them to think, not copy things down, during the model.
- Thinking processes are clearly narrated and they have made an active decision about whether they are modelling for 'coping' or 'mastery'.
- They ask more questions to check for understanding, and deeper process and probing questions.
- Scaffolds are provided as pupils begin more independent work and gradually removed as competence grows.

In GCSE PE, this could be a possible teaching sequence when introducing a class to 6 mark exam questions:

Q: Evaluate the importance of agility and reaction time for an 800m runner.

- Watch a video clip of an 800m and 400m elite race. Use mini whiteboards (MWBs) for pupils to highlight what is the same, what is different.
- In pairs, pupils identify an important component of fitness for each race. Q&A to dig into these. Pupils make a note of this info.
- Teacher models the same question but for a 400m runner, starting with a MWB knowledge check on already learned components of fitness definitions.
- Using the visualiser, the teacher selects a definition for reaction time from the class and talks through how this applies to the 400m, and crucially what the outcome is on the runner's performance, whilst showing the written work.
- Repeat for agility. The teacher asks the pupils to think through what they saw on the screen and write a sentence in their MWB about how agility relates to a 400m race. The teacher can give feedback on these and build this section of the answer with the class.
- Return now to those important components the pupils noted down earlier. Hopefully 'speed' was highlighted. The teacher can now narrate an evaluation of the relative importance of speed, agility and reaction time, and why in this case speed is vital.
- The pupils are now going to work on their version, same components, so some of the heavy lifting has been done, but relating to an 800m race.
- There's lots of other opportunities for check ins here if needed – more questions, more MWB tasks, or circulating the room and pausing to read out pupil work or deal with individual issues.
- As this is a first attempt, we're not aiming for exam-style total independence. Key Stage 3 pupils aren't used to writing for PE yet. We want all learners to feel confident to attempt this type of question. With this higher challenge, we give high support initially.

Dangerous assumptions

In education utopia, pupils choose a sport-related course at 14 years old because it fits their interests, hobbies and future career path. In real life, there are all sorts of reasons pupils choose courses or have courses chosen for them. The pupils in qualification PE classes aren't a homogenous bunch, so it's important not to jump to conclusions about what they will bring. Here are some potential assumptions that are worth considering carefully when planning for your 14–18 year old classes.

These pupils love sport, so they will watch sport/have good general knowledge of sport.

In my experience, this is definitely not true, especially for more disadvantaged catchments. I have used a pommel horse example and been met with very blank faces. Yet exam papers commonly refer to gymnastics events and athletics events as if these are common knowledge to pupils. So we need to make sure they are. We can share video clips and encourage pupils to watch sport and read about sport. In GCSE classes in my current setting, we try to watch at least one new event per fortnight in our theory lessons. Pole vault week is a big one!

Pupils will be able to identify the sports they should concentrate on for practical grades.

Pupils often assume that because they play a sport more regularly or it is their favourite, then it will be one of their highest scoring sports. Mindblowingly, they sometimes want this sport to be included in their NEA even when it is not high scoring. It's important to be up front about this early on; playing for a local football team may not be enough to secure a strong grade as per the GCSE specification, for example. It's also important that teachers examine the specifications and all their quirks – it is not always intuitive which skills appear on the prescribed lists.

Pupils will be able to transfer knowledge from other subjects, such as biology, into PE and vice versa.

This will only happen if you make the links clear and explicit to pupils. Build strong subject knowledge and work with other departments in your school to find out what topics link with PE content and when these are studied. Remember, don't leave these links to chance – only a few of the most competent learners will make them without you.

Pupils will be able to transfer extended writing skills from other subjects into PE.

We discussed in chapter 4 the riskiness of assuming that pupils will bring or connect thinking from one topic area to another. The same risk is present here: we need to teach pupils to write for PE.

Key takeaways

- Engage with exam board materials and CPD as much as you can – know your specification.
- Employ strategies to manage pupils' cognitive load, like pre-teaching vocabulary, using gestures and retaining similar task structures.
- Practise explanations and modelling sequences in advance.
- Plan scaffolds and small steps forward with more complex work. Far better to speed up and remove these quickly than to not have them ready and need to step backwards.

CHAPTER 10
MODE B IN PE

Moving away from instructional teaching in PE to give pupils different experiences is extremely important. One reason for this is that many physical activity opportunities for adults are not instructional in style. Another is that we need to give pupils the chance to be genuinely autonomous to support the development of physical literacy and their intrinsic motivation to be active. Handily, there are a lot of tools available for us to do this. At an informal level, we can give pupils choice over game structures and give responsibility for certain jobs. For example, in a Year 11 basketball unit of work, I commonly appoint a 'motivation captain' and a 'strategy captain' in each team – their jobs are fairly self-explanatory and I rotate the pupils regularly. Sometimes the team talks are wonderful! More formally, a number of 'models' for teaching PE are available to us, including Sport Education, Teaching Games for Understanding (TGFU), Tactical Games, Cooperative Learning, and Teaching Physical and Social Responsibility (TPSR). There is plenty of literature available to explore the models in more detail (including Casey and Kirk, 2021).

Getting started with models-based practice

Here we will spend more time thinking about what it might be like to implement models in your setting. To talk us through getting to grips with changing practice, I asked Ash Casey, Professor of Physical Education and Pedagogy at Loughborough University, some questions about his own journey as a PE teacher.

> **Q: For someone who is new to models-based practice, what's this all about?**
>
> A: The traditional organising centre for PE is the sport. Through that, there's a hope that other things might be taught, like leadership or cooperation. Models can create different organising centres for PE, so the activity becomes the vehicle to learn these other things.

Q: What was your starting point with models-based practice?

A: I came from a very stereotypical starting point. If you wanted to draw a pen portrait of a PE teacher, that was me. I was at a point where I was looking to do something differently. I had heard about models and started to do some reading. I chose to do an action research project with sport education and cricket in my school. It was working really well but the plug was pulled in my school so I didn't get to see where it might go. Next, I used tactical games, which I also found a good entry point for beginning to change my practice.

Q: What advice do you have for practitioners?

A: Remember that not only are you learning to teach in a different way, but pupils are also learning to learn in a different way. These two things are happening at the same time, so your decision making might not initially feel so fluent and your pupils may also be a little confused as they might not know how to be pupils in this new form of PE. Give yourself some time.

Don't be afraid to make a start, even if your initial programmes aren't completed faithfully to a named model. Remember that the way something lands in your school might be different to another school. Starting with a model that suits your situation can allow both staff and pupils to develop different ways of working; it can be easier to make changes in small steps.

Make your start easy. I started with Year 7 pupils, so sport education was the first thing they experienced. At the same time, if you have a difficult class and your existing approach isn't working, a change in practice could be worthwhile.

Finally, don't be afraid to use a scene-setting lesson zero. That investment in non-active time to introduce the unit and give clarity about the outcomes can result in increased activity a few lessons down the line.

Many readers will have heard of or delivered Sport Education units. It's great to hear Ash's recommendation that absolute fidelity to the model is not required and may not suit your context. In my current setting, we have a shorter, Sport Ed-lite unit in Year 9 so that pupils have the opportunity to experience and grow knowledge of the set up before they take real ownership of it in later years. I really enjoy delivering these units, in particular I love how it gives us the opportunity to celebrate contributions that aren't performance based. What a great way for even more pupils to feel even more successful in PE. How you engage with or deploy models will likely depend on your setting, your pupils and the expertise within the department.

Creating autonomy

Using a model like Sport Education gives pupils the opportunity to take on different roles and gives a certain amount of autonomy with that. In TGFU, you may be able to work with classes such that they identify and direct the next knowledge they need, through identifying a problem that has happened in their games. I find the more experience and more expertise pupils have, the better gains there are from the latter approach.

We can also give pupils a level of autonomy over the activity they study. Many schools offer 'pathways' of activities in Key Stage 4, where pupils choose a set of activities to study over a term. Another option is to 'negotiate' the curriculum with classes – involving pupils in setting out the activity and objectives in a unit of work (Aarksog et al, 2022; Guadelupe and Smith, 2019; 2020). I've experienced both; choosing options is like picking from a restaurant menu, whereas a negotiated curriculum is more like choosing the dish and identifying the ingredients. The latter feels like a more 'active' process. In any choice situation, avoid giving classes an 'either' 'or' which they then vote on. In this situation, some people 'lose' and their buy-in may be compromised. Try to secure interest in multiple options, consider omni-voting (you get multiple votes, so if you don't mind two of these options you vote for both), or work through discussion with the class.

Finally, there are times when we can give pupils real choices within lessons. This could be giving them the chance to set their own modification to a game or choose from some constraints you have already used. It could be that you give pupils the responsibility for carrying out a warm-up independently, but you have told them in advance what they need to get ready for. This is also a great recall and formative assessment opportunity – to what extent are pupils able to think through the actions or preparations that are most needed. A way I love to give pupils some freedom and choice in PE is to let them 'win' free play time. Let's say a class has a really great lesson. I will give some applied praise to say what has gone well, what we can now learn next, etc. I'll tell them they have won three minutes free play time at the start of the next lesson. They love this. That's right, they have exercised, been given more exercise, and it still feels like a win. In basketball for example, this free play time becomes the warm-up next lesson. What's great is that sometimes in this play time I see them trying out the stuff we have been learning, working together, and enjoying being with their classmates at school. That is well worth the three minutes.

Key takeaways

- Models can provide a different focus and way of working.
- Pick a path of least resistance to get going and build familiarity for you and the pupils.
- Lesson zeros make great scene setters, and a good chance to set the culture of how the unit will work.
- Other routes to provide autonomy include giving pupils choice over what they study. Try to do this through consensus; sometimes voting can divide.

CHAPTER 11
RELATIONSHIPS AND CULTURE

How teachers work with pupils is important in any subject. PE has some additional vulnerabilities: the performative nature; getting changed; society's structures around exercise. We also have the moral purpose of helping everyone move more and move better for life, not just for school PE. Whilst we cannot control this, we can hope to positively influence future behaviours through creating confidence and competence.

This is even more true for those with additional barriers to exercise. Maintaining a high expectation of what PE could and should look like for these pupils is vital.

In this section we will explore a range of teacher behaviours and choices that could create a positive environment for all learners. Developing a culture of mutual respect and supported risk-taking takes conscious thought and care. Without this, your well-designed curriculum or lesson won't pack the punch it could do.

Avoid...	Instead...
Using exercise as any kind of sanction, forfeit or punishment.	Create situations where exercise and active play are celebrated or are a reward (like the free play time mentioned in chapter 10).
Referring to pupils (or anyone) as being 'sporty' or 'talented'. If some people are these, then others are 'not sporty' or 'untalented'. PE is for everyone.	Be clear that you are sure that everyone can improve. Encourage pupils to compare their progress to their own previous performances. Celebrate genuine successes warmly.

Avoid...	Instead...
Setting a low bar for success. In my experience this can be a huge problem in girls' PE. Kind of an 'at least they are doing something' attitude. There can be similar issues for pupils with disabilities or other SEN. If you expect and demand less, that's exactly what you'll get.	Being aspirational for these groups starts with your curriculum planning. Be firm about what 'good' looks like, and plan the small steps and support needed for all pupils to be included and make progress. Sometimes this might be using different equipment (chapter 7), sometimes it might be thinking carefully about maximising involvement. For example, I often get a pupil who is struggling to be a scrum half in touch rugby. They are involved at every break down, get some thinking time to decide on run/pass/which pass, and get lots of touches on the ball. If they need more help, I can give them tackle protection (i.e. they can't be tagged) or put a confident communicator near them on the team.
Relating exercise to food or body size.	Exercise shouldn't be about guilt. Promote a positive relationship with movement by narrating the fun with friends, feel-good hormones, and satisfaction of making progress.
Using negative language in lessons: 'Stop being lazy! Keep up!' or 'Everyone else is trying hard.'	Narrate the positive: 'Well done to all those who are trying hard.' The pupil you see slowing down might still be doing their best. It's important to share with pupils how it feels to be out of breath and tired, and that most of the time that's ok and is temporary! We need them to trust that we will support them and never be a comic strip version of an unsympathetic autocrat PE teacher. We can be pupil cheerleaders while still holding them to account for their learning and conduct.

Avoid...	Instead...
Allowing a culture of criticism. Pupils can be quick to point out each other's mistakes. Lessons need to be safe spaces.	Model kindness in patience in your interactions. Remind them that no one ever gets up in the morning and thinks 'today I'd like to make a mistake that annoys my teammates'. Highlight other improvements in performances, or future opportunities. For example, we could say: 'Really crisp passing there team, and Adam was in a great space in the box. Show me another play to make a scoring chance. You know you can do it.' It also helps to not focus too much on scores. Mainly when I ask the pupils the score in mini games there are two purposes: Make sure the teams are even. As a starting point for a Q&A.
Rationing praise. It's not a finite resource!	Find opportunities for genuine praise and be clear about what the achievement is. Encourage pupils to praise each other. Tell your colleagues what they are doing well too. Another person doing something well doesn't mean you're doing it worse, and you might be able to learn something from them.

Getting to know your classes is one of the most fun bits of being a teacher. In PE we get those few minutes in the changing room where there might be a chance for an off-topic chat; finding out which pupils have pets, or love maths, or debate a big topic. Recently for me that's been samosas vs spring rolls (Year 7), and post-16 options (Year 11). This also helps with building belonging, an important part of developing intrinsic motivation. It can be nice to have a few things that are 'this is how we do this, in our class'. Maybe it's a little rule change in tag, or a way of doing the register line up. Or a shared joke, that everyone is in on. The more your classes feel like a team, the better. You can't have a PE lesson on your own.

A lot of this comes back to that big picture purpose. I would like as many pupils as possible to feel how I feel about exercise – that it is a vital part of life. I really hope when I bump into former pupils in town, they can tell me how they are keeping active. And I hope that this is at least in part because their PE lessons helped them to feel confident and competent enough to exercise.

Key takeaways

- You are the driver of culture in your classes. Hold high expectations for conduct and learning.
- Use praise to support pupil learning and confidence.
- Build belongings by treating your classes like teams.
- How pupils feel about PE is really important for both their school life and their whole life.

BIBLIOGRAPHY

Aarskog, E., Barker, D. and Spord Borgen, J. (2022). 'When it's something that you want to do', Exploring curriculum negotiation in Norwegian PE, *Physical Education and Sport Pedagogy*, 27(6), 640–53.

Association for Physical Education (2020). Health Position Paper. https://cdn.ymaws.com/afpe.site-ym.com/resource/resmgr/webinar_presenations/health-position-paper-2020-w.pdf.

Barton, C. (2017). 'Tick-Trash-Improve – Standard Form: TES Maths Resource of the Week', Mr Barton Maths Podcast. https://www.mrbartonmaths.com/blog/tick-trash-improve-standard-form-tes-maths-resource-of-the-week/.

Barton, C. (2022). *Tips for Teachers*. John Catt Educational.

Beale, N., Eldridge, E., Delextrat, A., Esser, P., Bushnell, O., Curtis, E., Wassenaar, T., Wheatly, C., Johansen-Berg, H. and Dawes, H. (2021). 'Exploring activity levels in physical education lessons in the UK: a cross-sectional examination of activity types and fitness levels', *BMJ Open Sport & Exercise Medicine*, 7(1).

Bernstein, E., Phillips, S. R. and Silverman, S. (2011). 'Attitudes and perceptions of middle school students toward competitive activities in physical education', *Journal of Teaching in Physical Education*, 30(1), 69–83.

Bjork, E. L. and Bjork, R. A. (2011). 'Making things hard on yourself, but in a good way: Creating desirable difficulties to enhance learning', in M. A. Gernsbacher, R. W. Pew, L. M. Hough & J. R. Pomerantz (eds), *Psychology and the real world: Essays illustrating fundamental contributions to society* (pp. 56–54). Worth Publishers.

Casey, A. and Kirk, D. (2021). *Models-based Practice in Physical Education*. Routledge.

Chow, J. Y., Komar, J., and Seifert, L. (2021). 'The role of nonlinear pedagogy in supporting the design of modified games in junior sports', *Frontiers in Psychology*, 12, Article 744814.

Croston, A. (2014). 'The construction and experience of ability in physical education' [PhD thesis, Brunel University]. https://bura.brunel.ac.uk/handle/2438/8433.

Deci, E. L. and Ryan, R. M. (2000). 'The "What" and "Why" of Goal Pursuits: Human Needs and the Self-Determination of Behavior', *Psychological Inquiry*, 11(4), 227–68.

Delextrat, A., Esser, P., Beale, N., Bozon, F., Eldridge, E., Izadi, H., Johansen-Berg, H., Wheatley, C. and Dawes, H. (2020). 'Effects of gender, activity type, class location and class composition on physical activity levels experienced during physical education classes in British secondary schools: a pilot cross-sectional study', *BMC Public Health*, 20, 1590.

Department for Education (2023). Levelling the playing field: the physical education subject report. https://www.gov.uk/government/publications/subject-report-series-pe/levelling-the-playing-field-the-physical-education-subject-report#secondary-findings.

Education Endowment Foundation (2021). Teaching and Learning toolkit. Setting and streaming. https://educationendowmentfoundation.org.uk/education-evidence/teaching-learning-toolkit/setting-and-streaming.

Galán, I., Boix, R., Medrano, M. J., Ramos, P., Rivera, F., Pastor-Barriuso, R. and Moreno, C. (2013). 'Physical activity and self-reported health status among adolescents: a cross-sectional population-based study', *BMJ Open*, 3.

Gray, R. (2021). *How We Learn to Move: A Revolution in the Way We Coach & Practice Sports Skills*, Perception Action Consulting & Education LLC.

Gray, R. (2022). *Learning to Optimise Movement*. Independently published.

Guadalupe, T. and Curtner-Smith, M. D. (2019). 'She was really good at letting us make decisions: influence of purposefully negotiating the physical education curriculum on one teacher and a boys' middle school minority class', *Curriculum Studies in Health and Physical Education*, 10(2), 109–25.

Guadalupe, T. and Curtner-Smith, M. D. (2020). 'It's nice to have choices: influence of purposefully negotiating the curriculum on the students in one mixed-gender middle school class and their teacher', *Sport, Education and Society*, 25(8), 904–16.

Heath, C. and Heath D. (2007). *Made to Stick: Why some ideas survive and others die* (1st ed). Random House.

Howard, T. (2023). 'Practical, professional or patriarchal? An investigation into the socio-cultural impacts of gendered school sports uniform and the role uniform plays in shaping female experiences of school sport', *Sport, Education and Society*, 1–18.

Ives, H. and Kirk, D. (2012). 'What are the public perceptions of physical education?' in S. Capel (ed) *Debates in Physical Education*. Routledge.

Johnson, M. and Ward, P. (2001). 'Effects of classwide peer tutoring on correct performance of striking skills in 3rd grade physical education', *Journal of Teaching in Physical Education*, 20, 247–63.

Kegelaers, J. and Sarkar, M. (2021). 'Psychological resilience in high-performance athletes: Elucidating some common myths and misconceptions', in A. Whitehead & J. Coe (ed) *Myths of Sport Coaching* (pp. 234–46).

Lemov, D. (2020). *The Coach's Guide to Teaching*. John Catt Educational.

Lemov, D. (2021). *Teach Like a Champion 3.0: 63 Techniques That Put Students on the Path to College*. Jossey-Bass.

Lindsay, R. and Spittle, M. (2024). 'The adaptable coach – a critical review of the practical implications for traditional and constraints-led approaches in sport coaching', *International Journal of Sports Science and Coaching*, 19(3), pp. 1240–54.

McCrea, P. (2020). *Motivated Teaching*. High Impact Teaching.

McGrane, C. (2020). *Mathematical Tasks: The Bridge Between Teaching and Learning*. John Catt Educational.

O'Connor, J., Alfrey, L. and Penney, D. (2022). 'Rethinking the classification of games and sports in physical education: a response to changes in sport and participation', *Physical Education and Sport Pedagogy*, 29(3), 315–28.

O'Connor, J. and Penney, D. (2021). 'Informal sport and curriculum futures: An investigation of the knowledge, skills and understandings for participation and the possibilities for physical education', *European Physical Education Review*, 27(1), 3–26.

Rosenshine, B. (2012). 'Principles of instruction: Research-based strategies that all teachers should know', *American Educator*, 36(1), 12–39.

Sherrington, T. (2019). *Rosenshine's Principles in Action*. John Catt Educational.

Soderstrom, N. C. and Bjork, R. A. (2015). 'Learning Versus Performance: An Integrative Review', *Perspectives on Psychological Science*, 10(2), 176–99.

Sport England (2023a). Physical Literacy Consensus Statement for England published, 28 September. https://www.sportengland.org/news-and-inspiration/physical-literacy-consensus-statement-england-published.

Sport England (2023b). Active Lives Adult Survey November 2021-22 Report.

Turner, E., Goodwin, D., and Caviglioli, O. (2022). *Annie Murphy Paul's The Extended Mind in Action*. John Catt Educational.

Urhahne, D. and Wijnia, L. (2023). 'Theories of Motivation in Education: an Integrative Framework', *Educational Psychology Review*, 35, 45.

Visek A. J., Achrati S. M., Mannix, H., McDonnell, K., Harris, B. S., DiPietro, L. (2015). 'The fun integration theory: toward sustaining children and adolescents sport participation', *Journal of Physical Activity and Health*, 12(3), 424–33.

Wallace, L., Buchan, D. and Sculthorpe, N. (2020). 'A comparison of activity levels of girls in single-gender and mixed-gender physical education', *European Physical Education Review*, 26(1), 231–40.

Ward, K., Hastie, P. and Strunk, K. (2018). 'Effects of Ability Grouping on Students' Game Performance and Physical Activity. *Journal of Teaching in Physical Education*.

White, R., Bennie, A., Vasconcellos, D., Cinelli, R., Hilland, T., Owen, K. and Lonsdale, C. (2020). 'Self-determination theory in physical education: A systematic review of qualitative studies', *Teaching and Teacher Education*, 99.

Whitehead, A. and Coe, J. (2021). *Myths of Sport Coaching*. Sequoia.

Wilkinson, S. D., Penney, D., Allin, L., and Potrac, P. (2021). 'The enactment of setting policy in secondary school physical education', *Sport, Education and Society*, 26(6), 619–33.

Wilkinson, S. D. and Penney, D. (2022). 'The participation group means that I'm low ability: Students' perspectives on the enactment of 'mixed-ability' grouping in secondary school physical education', *British Educational Research Journal*, 48, 932–51.

Women's Sport and Fitness Foundation (2012). *Changing the Game for Girls*. Report.

World Health Organization (2020). *WHO Guidelines on physical activity and sedentary behaviour*. Geneva: World Health Organization.

Wright, D. and Kim, T. (2019). 'Contextual interference', *Skill Acquisition in Sport*, 3rd edition.

Youth Sport Trust (2019). Assessing without levels in PE. Version 3.

Youth Sport Trust (2023) 'Girls Active programme'. https://www.youthsporttrust.org/programmes/targeted-interventions/girls-active.